Homes for All
Serving People with Disabilities

Robert Davies and
Merrill Black

Developed in conjunction
with the New York State
Association of REALTORS®, Inc.

Dearborn
Real Estate Education

President: Roy Lipner
Vice President of Product Development & Publishing: Evan M. Butterfield
Managing Editor: Kate DeVivo
Senior Development Editor: Anne Huston
Director of Production: Daniel Frey
Production Editor: Samantha Raue
Production Artist: Virginia Byrne
Creative Director: Lucy Jenkins

Published by Dearborn™ Real Estate Education
30 South Wacker Drive
Chicago, Illinois 60606-7481
(312) 836-4400
www.dearbornRE.com

Printed in the United States of America

07 08 09 10 9 8 7 6 5 4 3 2 1

contents

Chapter 4   **Accessibility Issues   34**

Chapter 5   **Strategies for Reaching People with Disabilities   42**

Chapter 6   **Case Studies   51**

Merrill Black, president of the writing and training firm Active Voice, was the first national coordinator of the National Home of Your Own Alliance. She is the co-author, with Alliance founder Jay Klein, of *Extending the American Dream: Home Ownership for People with Disabilities*. She has over 25 years experience working with nonprofit organizations whose missions involve affordable housing, community economic development, health care, and education.

Robert (Rob) Davies has worked in the field of disabilities for the past 33 years, primarily in developmental disabilities. He is a consultant to individuals, families, local, regional, state, national, and international organizations and governments. He is a frequent speaker at state, national, and international meetings, conferences, and educational seminars on disability and senior issues. He is the former director of housing initiatives for the New York State Office of Mental Retardation and Developmental Disabilities where he developed rental subsidy programs for persons with developmental disabilities and traumatic brain injuries; mortgage products in conjunction with Fannie Mae, the National Home of Your Own Alliance, and the State of New York Mortgage Agency; and initiatives in supplemental needs trusts and family-initiated housing options.

People with disabilities comprise the largest minority in the United States; approximately one in every six Americans has a disability. Yet they are largely overlooked as a market for the real estate industry. Serving people with disabilities can be a satisfying way to focus your business while elevating the public's perception of the real estate industry.

This course will raise your awareness about the disability community. You will learn about the Independent Living Movement, which has allowed thousands of people with disabilities to move from agency-run facilities into their own homes. You will learn to build relationships with people who have disabilities and those who support them.

"The greatest disability that adults with disabilities face is poverty," according to disability housing expert and former realtor Derrick Dufresne of Community Resource Associates, and this course will make you aware of resources and mortgage products to help those on a limited budget attain homeownership. The course's approach of blending all resources to qualify an individual with disabilities will assist anyone interested in creative financing. You can also apply much of what you learn here to expand into the broader market of first-time homebuyers who are looking for affordable housing.

In the current real estate market, it's good to know that there is an untapped market of buyers with both the capacity and the enthusiasm for homeownership. This course presents an opportunity to broaden your knowledge as an agent and to find a new revenue stream from a market interested in accessible housing, a market that will continue to grow as the general population ages. Throughout these chapters and the case studies in Chapter 6, you will gain an insight into what it takes to effectively reach people with disabilities, a niche market that presents real estate professionals with a growing opportunity for steady income, repeat business, and an enjoyable career.

Homes for All: Serving People with Disabilities would not have been possible without the thoughtful feedback of real estate professionals and disability specialists. The authors wish to thank the following individuals for their manuscript reviews and contributions to the course:

- Stephen Beard, REALTOR®, Keller Williams Realty, Oakland, CA
- Sheila Bell, Sheila Bell Seminars, Cincinnati, OH
- Derrick Dufresne, senior partner, Community Resource Alliance, St. Louis, MO
- Jim Kessler, director, Department of Disability Services, University of North Carolina, Chapel Hill; past-president, Association on Higher Education and Disability

1

Overview of a Market: People with Disabilities

Learning Objectives

After completing this chapter, you will be able to

- Detail the demographics of this growing market

- Identify the reasons people with disabilities meet criteria for "good prospects"

- List milestones in policy and practice leading to the growth of this client base

- List considerations that impact your serving those clients

- Explain how serving this population is part of a strategy to grow your business and improve public perception of the real estate industry

■ Key Terms

Americans with
  Disabilities Act (ADA)

budget-based qualifying

Community Home
  Choice™ program

Federal Fair Housing Act

Independence Plus

Independent Living
  Movement

Money Follows the Person

National Home of Your
  Own Alliance

New Freedom Initiative

nontraditional sources of
  income

representative payee

self-determination

■ Demographics

As a real estate licensee, you are in a position to make the American dream of homeownership available to a significant and growing underserved group—the estimated 49 million–plus Americans with some type of disability. People with disabilities have wages or other forms of income that can qualify them as homebuyers.

According to the 2002 Census

- about 56 percent of Americans with disabilities, ages 21 to 64, had jobs; and
- about 43 percent of adults with severe disabilities had jobs.

Builders, architects, real estate professionals, bankers, and mortgage brokers can benefit from learning more about this motivated and qualified market of buyers, particularly in the current environment, because these buyers have the resources and willingness to buy and are eligible for the special lending products this course will teach you about. Many people with disabilities, including those with significant physical and intellectual disabilities, are looking for accessible, affordable houses and are arranging for individualized support services in their new homes. Learning how to serve this niche can help you serve both the aging market and the growing pool of low and medium income first-time homebuyers. It can also expand your awareness of resources in your community, elevate public perception of the real estate industry, and bring a new form of personal satisfaction to your career.

No doubt you've heard of the **Americans with Disabilities Act (ADA)** and the **Federal Fair Housing Act**. You may be less aware of the **Independent Living Movement** behind these laws, a forty-year-old movement that has led more people with disabilities to be far more likely to become homeowners. In 2002, nearly one in six Americans had some form of disability, according to the Census Bureau. About 33 million had severe disabilities that were expected to be lifelong. More than 50 percent of those aged 65 and older, and 72 percent of those aged 80 and older, have disabilities. The information in this course is critical to your serving an aging population.

When you consider the nearly 50 million Americans with some type of disability, along with others often involved in their home purchase—their family members and support staff—you are approaching a market of well over 150 million people potentially interested in buying homes. As parents age, they often become highly motivated to use their assets to secure permanent, safe housing for their adult children with disabilities through homeownership.

Today, agencies serving people with disabilities are mandated to move people into community settings and often have programs to secure homeownership for their clients. In this transition toward more integrated settings, institutions such as group homes and nursing homes often serve clients who are eligible for homeownership and have the means to become homeowners. In 2004, disability lawyers estimated there were over 200,000 people nationally living in nursing homes who were actively seeking community-based alternatives, including homeownership.

A real estate professional who works successfully with a person with a disability can expect positive referrals. Agency staff and family members are active in support groups with other families affected by disability and have individual networks where good news spreads quickly. Several real estate professionals profiled in this course talk about the rewards of working with this underserved market. Many members of this new market do not have any special needs in terms of accessibility while others may need accessible homes, staff support, or special modifications to make their home work for them.

California real estate licensee Stephen Beard, profiled later in this course, says, "With a consistent, methodical approach and a sound business plan, a real estate professional who truly wants to serve this market can make a successful business doing it."

■ People with Disabilities Are Good Prospects

We all want some form of special accommodation when we look for a home; it may be a large garage, proximity to the commuter train, or lots of natural light. A person with a disability is no different in the basic desire of wanting a safe, affordable home that meets his or her needs. People who need additional accommodation because of limitations in mobility or other areas often have difficulty finding accessible homes. When they find what they need, they quickly take advantage of the opportunity and will be happy to refer others to the real estate professional who helped them. In short, they are good prospects. A good prospect has:

- the financial capacity and a steady source of income;
- the ability to make decisions or to have someone to make decisions for them (guardian or power of attorney);
- a clear idea of what he or she wants; and
- the willingness to generate referrals and repeat business.

Examining this niche market in terms of these criteria provides a general overview of what you will learn in this course, introduces you to some new terms, and challenges some assumptions you might have.

Financial Capacity and a Steady Source of Income

While many people with disabilities are fully employed, many are eligible for public entitlements such as Supplemental Security Income (SSI) and Social Security Disability Insurance (SSDI). Procedures are now in place to qualify buyers for mortgages using **nontraditional sources of income**, such as SSI and SSDI benefits. Medical needs and critical personal support (home health aides, personal attendants, etc.) are often paid for through Medicaid.

Banks are increasingly convinced that these income sources from benefits programs are as reliable over time as income from employment. In this type of **budget-based qualifying,** the decision is made not on earned income and credit, but on a budget that includes the person's monthly benefits. In addition to special mortgage products from Fannie Mae, there are also state and local agencies that provide programs and resources to people with disabilities, thus enabling them to meet the first criteria for a good prospect. Chapter 3 contains a detailed discussion of these income streams and financing sources.

Ability to Make Decisions

Some people with disabilities make all their own decisions; others do not. Sometimes support agencies, representative payees, or guardians handle bill payment and other financial decisions. This issue is significant when considering buying a home because an agency or an individual appointed by Social Security may act as the buyer's **representative payee**; in which case, the agency or individual would provide crucial documentation for the mortgage application, and may, in some cases, contribute to either the down payment or the monthly mortgage payment.

In a few cases, you may be dealing with a person's guardian or with a trustee of a special needs trust. A guardian is legally designated to make financial and other major decisions on behalf of the person with a disability. The asset limitations allow for special needs trusts for home purchase or other special purposes to be set up for people with disabilities. If your client has a guardian or trustee, he or she will apply to the court to be able to close on the house in the person's name. A trustee of a special needs trust has the discretion to make appropriate payments for housing expenses.

The independent living movement has helped people with disabilities be more visible and more vocal about their rights to participate fully in society, and legislation has mandated greater consumer choice and involvement in the services they receive from agencies. **Self-determination** in the decision-making process for persons with severe disabilities is a national movement today and a best practice in the service provision industry. Self-determination means that people with disabilities, with their relatives and paid support staff members, drive the decision making rather than the professional support staff at the agency that serves them. Over the past few years this trend has radically changed the way agencies do business and has implications for homeownership as self-determination dictates that consumers—the people with disabilities—have more control over how the benefits they receive through entitlement programs are allocated.

Clear Idea of What They Want

Factors such as proximity to services and family, accessibility, and price are critical to people with disabilities, as they are for many homebuyers. If the person uses a wheelchair, curb cuts and accessible transportation will also be important. If the person relies on an agency, family, or friends for services, properties within a fixed geographic radius will be identified. A person with a disability sometimes has had to spend more time learning how to navigate the world, so he or she may have a clearer idea of what they want than a buyer without disabilities who says, "I will know it when I see it."

New MLS Screen.   Indicative of the growing interest in this market, some MLS Web sites have added a new screen with more detailed fields to offer more information on what a house listed as "accessible" really features. In one New York MLS region, 13 descriptive attributes are available when the Handicap Access field is answered yes. Two regional MLS listings in the area served by California REALTOR® Stephen Beard include a detailed set of accessibility features that can be used by agents to describe a home. Beard is designing a database of accessible properties, and hopes to organize a national network of real estate professionals experienced with working with people with disabilities (see *www.accessiblerealtor network.com*).

In areas where the MLS supports more detail on accessibility features, salespersons are better able to select properties for preview that meet their clients' needs, and they can better customize the search for properties. Where such services exist, it is important that salespersons complete the fields properly to effectively share accessibility information. While MLS search criteria pertaining to accessibility is useful, in many areas the stock of accessible housing is quite low, so a more typical search involves locating a home that meets the prospective buyer's approval and then exploring ways to modify the property to make it fully accessible.

Willingness to Generate Referrals and Repeat Business

According to real estate agent Peter Staniels, profiled later in this chapter, by the time you have been in business five years, ideally 75 percent of your business is coming from referrals and repeat business. This is an area where having some success in marketing to people with disabilities can help build your business and strengthen your reputation as an involved and caring community member.

Local agencies that work with people with disabilities are under increasing pressure to find housing for their clients, and in many cases homeownership is the solution with the best outcome. For busy agency staff, finding a real estate professional who is comfortable communicating with persons with disabilities and has some sense of accessibility needs would be the "one-stop shop" they've been looking for.

As a property manager or a buyer's agent for people with disabilities, you could market your services to service provider agencies and parent groups and expect a solid response. The parent who has a positive experience with you in buying a home for their adult child may belong to a number of parent networks and would be happy to refer their friends to you for their own child's housing needs.

Because you often have relationships with developers, you are in a position to influence those who create housing stock. By becoming comfortable with the principles of universal design (Chapter 4), you can make a positive contribution toward ensuring that the housing available in the 21st century reflects the needs of both the aging population and persons with disabilities. In marketing to people with disabilities, you can augment your business (and the public perception of the real estate industry) and build a strong stream of referrals by meeting the needs of this enormous untapped market.

New York salesperson Peter Staniels shares his experiences serving the disability market.

Industry Profile: Realty Firm Establishes Special Needs Department

Peter Staniels
Weichert Realtors® Northeast Group
Albany, NY

I looked at the market from a business perspective and saw an underserved, underutilized market. Some of the product that we had that was difficult to sell turned out to be ideal for people with disabilities, such as one family home on a bus line and one located in a commercial district.

One real estate transaction in particular was an epiphany for me and got me thinking about additional opportunities. One of our agents listed a house that had been completely modified for a person who used a wheelchair. At that time we had no methodology for getting this information to the disability market. Ultimately, we ended up selling it to a client who eventually tore all the modifications out. "What a waste," we thought. With all the time, effort, and money that went into the home, it actually became a liability to the person who bought it. From that time on, whenever we receive a property that is specialized, we dedicate ourselves to finding a buyer to whom these specializations will be valuable.

(continued)

We have now set up a small special-needs department within our firm, focusing on housing issues affecting people with disabilities. One of our first steps was to go to our regional board of REALTORS® whose MLS did not offer the option to select any specific types of accommodations or accessibility features at all other than "Handicapped Access, Yes or No." We developed about a dozen descriptive field options, and both agents and clients can search the database.

We'd like to go even further, where houses that have been modified or reflect universal design could be designated as such and made explicitly available in a national or state MLS. It could be funded with a user fee from the seller and administered by local building departments. If it could be done nationally, it would be a great assistance when people with disabilities move or relocate. Such a designation would be of value for the seller who would be more likely to get his asking price, and the buyer who would benefit by being able to more easily locate specialized housing. Some states, such as Massachusetts, Virginia, and Nevada, have a database of accessible rental housing—why not take it further?

Our industry could do more for housing people with disabilities than ever before if every agent did just one transaction a year. How could this be achieved? First, there should be a national database of accessible housing that is correctly categorized and that licensees and clients could tap into. On the financial side, there should be a real coordinated effort in the banking community to have programs available on an ongoing basis, and to get the message out about these programs. Salespersons and prospective purchasers must still do this research—there is not yet a national clearinghouse of financial opportunities. Second, there must be a continuing public relations campaign to let agents know this market exists and that it would serve us well to get involved. All the franchises have national conventions—one or more breakout sessions should be on serving people with disabilities. A national designation for serving people with disabilities should be developed, and there could be several designated experts in every community.

■ The Road to Independent Living

For an overall perspective on this market, we turn to milestones along the road to independent living. In the United States during the 1960s, community care laws and the civil rights movement began the deinstitutionalization process for many people with disabilities. During the 1970s, a number of class action suits to end the appalling treatment in state schools and institutions led to the development of community housing such as group homes. Real estate professionals began to work with nonprofit agencies serving people with disabilities to assist in the purchase and development of these options.

In 1973 Congress passed the Rehabilitation Act and the term reasonable accommodation came into use—the concept that all programs receiving federal funding must accommodate people with disabilities in obtaining housing, education, employment, and other areas supported by public funds, so that people were not discriminated against or denied a role in society by virtue of their disability.

State and Local Agencies

During the late 1970s and throughout the 1980s many institutions were closed and people with disabilities moved into various community housing opportunities. A network of nonprofit agencies serving people with disabilities began operating to provide support services and, sometimes, group homes and other forms of housing. Increasingly, these agencies are interested in homeownership for their clients and can be an important part of this growing market.

Each state has a network of regional offices, usually administered by the state Health and Human Services Department, which contract with local providers to support people with disabilities in securing housing, employment, training, and health care. Additionally, all states have federally funded planning councils, such as the Developmental Disabilities Planning Council (DDPC) and the University Institutes on Disability (UID) with the mission of researching and implementing innovative programming for people with disabilities. Also, there are independent living centers throughout the United States that provide resources and services and are often run by people with disabilities. Researching these networks will help you learn more and reach out to this growing market.

Through the advocacy and research of these networks, services in the 1990s became more flexibly structured, funded, and individualized so that people with disabilities could become active members of a more inclusive society. While a great number of persons with disabilities live with family members, many are living in small group homes, supported and supervised apartments, or in their own homes, apartments, condos, or co-ops.

National Home of Your Own Alliance

In the early 1990s the federal Administration on Developmental Disabilities (ADD) funded a national project, the National Home of Your Own Alliance, to demonstrate that disability and affordable housing networks could work with conventional lenders to expand the options for homeownership for people with disabilities. The Alliance was a partnership between the federal government and nationally recognized advocates and leaders whose goal was to create housing and support opportunities for people with disabilities through statewide initiatives. It was a major step in providing options for people with disabilities. Real estate professionals played key roles in several member states.

As a result of the National Home of Your Own Alliance project, thirty-five states in the United States now have homeownership initiatives. In Milwaukee, for instance, IndependenceFirst has established a homeownership program for low-income persons with disabilities. Some 200 new homeowners have been assisted in their home purchase and there have been no known loan defaults for any of the homeowners. Co-op Initiatives, a program in New Haven, Connecticut, administers a down payment assistance program and maintains a registry of accessible housing. New York State, under the leadership of the New York Office of Mental Retardation and Developmental Disability, has assisted hundreds of people with disabilities to purchase their own homes by establishing a mortgage product for persons with mental and developmental disabilities. The mortgage is a 30-year fixed at 4 percent with no down payment through the State of New York Mortgage Agency (SONYMA).

Other Programs

Banks and federal, state, and local housing and disability agencies have developed a number of new programs and mortgage products to serve the market. Fannie Mae's **Community HomeChoice**™ provides special underwriting to meet the needs of low- to moderate-income borrowers with disabilities, or those who have a family member with a disability. Individual states, like New York and California, have developed mortgage products through their housing finance agencies and local lenders based on the Fannie Mae product. See *www.ncsha.org* to locate your state's Housing Finance Authority or for a comprehensive list of disability resources by state.

◼ The Independent Living Movement

Figure 1.1 outlines key events leading to the Independent Living Movement. Legislation as well as community response has made a vast difference in how those with disabilities are understood and the niche market open to real estate salespersons who are willing to learn, research, and reach out with opportunities.

Since 1996, the Robert Wood Johnson Foundation has funded nationwide grants to increase the use of the theories and practices of self-determination to change service delivery in the field of developmental disabilities. This has assisted states and communities in transitioning to systems of support that recognize people's abilities rather than their disabilities.

In 1999, the Supreme Court issued the Olmstead decision requiring states to administer their services, programs, and activities "in the most integrated setting appropriate to the needs of qualified individuals with disabilities." Since then more people are applying the benefits they are entitled to towards homeownership, and more agencies serving people with disabilities are helping their clients buy homes.

In 2001, President George W. Bush signed an executive order to implement the **New Freedom Initiative**, a comprehensive plan to ensure that all Americans have the opportunity to learn and develop skills, engage in productive work, make choices about their daily lives, and participate fully in community life. The Initiative's goals are to

- ◼ increase access to assistive and universally designed technologies;
- ◼ expand educational opportunities;
- ◼ promote homeownership;
- ◼ integrate Americans with disabilities into the workforce;
- ◼ expand transportation options; and
- ◼ promote full access to community life.

The **Independence Plus** initiative, in which the Department of Health and Human Services (DHHS) promised to provide states with simplified model waiver and demonstration application templates to promote person-centered planning and self-directed service options, was initiated in 2002. Following this, **Money Follows the Person** began as part of the New Freedom Initiative to assist persons transitioning from nursing homes to their own home. It also assists in diverting persons from entering nursing homes or other institutions to living in the community in their own homes.

Figure 1.1 | Timeline of Independent Living Movement

1961
- President Kennedy appoints special President's Panel on Mental Retardation to develop programs and reforms.
- The American National Standards Institute, Inc. (ANSI) publishes American Standard Specifications for Making Buildings Accessible to, and Usable by, the Physically Handicapped.

1963
- President Kennedy asks that methods be found "to retain in and return to the community the mentally ill and mentally retarded, and there to restore and revitalize their lives through better health programs and strengthened educational and rehabilitation services."
- Congress passes the Mental Retardation Facilities and Community Health Centers Construction Act.

1964
- Passage of the Civil Rights Act outlawing discrimination on the basis of race in public accommodations, employment, and federally assisted programs. The Civil Rights Act of 1964 will become a model for subsequent disability rights legislation.
- The "acoustic coupler," forerunner of the telephone modem, is invented.

1965
- Medicare and Medicaid are established through passage of the Social Security Amendments of 1965.
- Vocational Rehabilitation Amendments of 1965 are passed, authorizing federal grants for the construction of rehabilitation centers, expanding existing programs, and creating the National Commission on Architectural Barriers to Rehabilitation of the Handicapped.

1968
- The Architectural Barriers Act is passed, mandating that federally constructed buildings and facilities be accessible to people with physical disabilities.

1970
- Congress passes the Urban Mass Transportation Assistance Act, declaring it a "national policy that elderly and handicapped persons have the same right as other persons to utilize mass transportation facilities and services."

1972
- The Center for Independent Living is founded in Berkeley, California. Generally recognized as the world's first independent living center, sparking the worldwide independent living movement.
- Passage of the Social Security Amendments of 1972 creates the Supplemental Security Income (SSI) program.

1973
- Passage of the Rehabilitation Act of 1973 confronts discrimination against people with disabilities. Section 504 prohibits programs receiving federal funds from discriminating against "otherwise qualified handicapped" individuals.

1974
- North Carolina passes a statewide building code with stringent access requirements. This becomes a model for effective architectural access legislation in other states.

1975
- The Education for All Handicapped Children Act (or P.L. 94 - 142) is passed establishing the right of children with disabilities to a public school education in an integrated environment.

1986
- The Employment Opportunities for Disabled Americans Act is passed allowing recipients of SSI and SSDI to retain benefits, including medical coverage, even after they obtain work.

1988
- The Technology-Related Assistance Act for Individuals with Disabilities (the "Tech Act") is passed, authorizing federal funding to state projects designed to facilitate access to assistive technology.
- The Fair Housing Amendments Act adds people with disabilities to those groups protected by federal fair housing legislation, and establishes minimum standards of access and adaptability for newly constructed multiple-dwelling housing.

1989
- The Center for Universal Design (originally the Center for Accessible Housing) is founded in North Carolina.

1990
- President George H. W. Bush signs the Americans with Disabilities Act (ADA). The law mandates that local, state, and federal governments and programs be accessible, that businesses with more than 15 employees make "reasonable accommodations" for workers with disabilities, and that public accommodations make "reasonable modifications" to ensure access for people with disabilities. The Act also mandates that public transportation, communication, and other areas of public life be accessible.
- The ADA, though primarily affecting commercial and industrial accommodation, also has a residential housing component. That component requires that condominium builders set aside 5 percent of their new developments for people with disabilities.

Adapted from *ABC-CLIO Companion to The Disability Rights Movement*, by Fred Pelka. ABC-CLIO: Santa Barbara, 1997.

■ Chapter 1 Review Questions

1. Which statement best explains what makes people with disabilities a viable real estate target market?

   a. Many people with some type of disability have significant income.

   b. People with disabilities make up approximately 18 percent of the population.

   c. There are governmental programs to assist persons with disabilities become homeowners.

   d. All of the above

2. Homeownership is most beneficial to a person with a disability because

   a. an institution is not a good place to live.

   b. it provides long-term, stable, and individualized housing.

   c. homeownership builds equity.

   d. everyone should be a homeowner.

3. How will working with clients with disabilities be most likely to enhance your business?

   a. It saves taxpayers' money.

   b. It creates client loyalty and additional business opportunities.

   c. It could cause neighborhood opposition, which would help publicize your business.

   d. It familiarizes you with a new market.

4. Not factoring in families and support, the market for serving people with some form of disability is approximately

   a. 50 million people.

   b. 25 million people.

   c. 150 million people.

   d. 75 million people.

5. Which factor contributes to the growth of the population of people with disabilities?

   a. More babies are born with disabilities.

   b. Doctors are classifying more people as having disabilities.

   c. People are living longer.

   d. More people have autism.

6. Office ABC, a nonprofit business, has 18 employees, one of whom uses a wheelchair. The president of the company refuses to pay for the installation of a wheelchair ramp. He is in violation of the

   a. Employment Opportunities for Disabled Americans Act.

   b. Americans with Disabilities Act.

   c. Rehabilitation Act.

   d. Fair Housing Act.

7. People with disabilities were added as a new protected class to those groups protected by fair housing legislation in the

   a. Fair Housing Amendments Act of 1988.

   b. Vocational Rehabilitation Amendments of 1965.

   c. Rehabilitation Act of 1973.

   d. Americans with Disabilities Act of 1990.

8. Fannie Mae's mortgage product that provides special underwriting to meet the needs of people with disabilities is called

   a. First Home Club.

   b. Home of Your Own.

   c. IndependenceFirst.

   d. Community HomeChoice™.

9. Budget-based qualifying is

   a. not accepted by mortgage lenders.

   b. qualifying based on all sources of income both private and public.

   c. a qualifying procedure used by new homeowners.

   d. an age-old technique in qualifying new homeowners.

10. Can the Internet and MLS be useful in finding accessible housing?

    a. Not usually, because accessibility information is not accurate.

    b. No, because Internet information cannot be trusted.

    c. Yes, because many Internet listings and MLS services have accessibility information.

    d. Only MLS information is accurate.

2

Understanding Disabilities: People First

Learning Objectives

After completing this chapter, you will be able to

■ Name and understand different types of disabilities

■ List common accommodations for different disabilities

■ Use appropriate language and behaviors to communicate successfully with persons with disabilities

■ Identify individuals who might be involved in decision making for home purchase and describe their roles

■ Key Terms

accommodation

assistive technology
  device

court-appointed guardian

independent living center

participation

people first

people first language

trustee

■ Introduction

Relating to people with disabilities generally follows the same rules as relating to anyone else. People appreciate respect and courtesy no matter what their age, I.Q., or physical status/ability. As a general rule, it is always better to ask than to presume that a person needs help or can't do something. **People first** refers to the part of the disability rights movement that asserts that people are defined by their humanity first, not by their disability, so, for example, it is more respectful to say "a person with a disability" than to refer to "a disabled person" or to groups of people with disabilities aggregated by their condition as in phrases like "the blind," "the deaf," "the disabled."

The Americans with Disabilities Act (ADA) defines disability as "a physical or mental impairment that substantially limits a major life activity, such as walking, seeing, hearing, learning, breathing, caring for oneself, or working." People without disabilities are sometimes uncomfortable around people with disabilities, afraid they are saying or doing the wrong thing. As a real estate licensee, you should ask yourself regularly, "How can we make this work?" People with disabilities and the people around them often develop this same problem-solving attitude that helps them accommodate for the limits imposed by their disability. Knowing a little more about the categories of disabilities can help you prepare to accommodate your client in ways that can make both of you more comfortable and able to work together more effectively. Each person is unique. While there is no one way to serve this community, this chapter will raise your awareness so you can tailor your approach to your prospective buyer's circumstances.

There is a natural course of disability that often accompanies aging, and all of us make accommodations for this. We begin to experience hearing and sight loss in middle age. We can no longer read the fine print and suddenly it seems like everyone is mumbling. Opening that jar or climbing those stairs becomes harder. We forget what we were saying halfway through the sentence. So we make accommodations: we get glasses, ask people to repeat themselves, take the stairs more slowly, place higher-intensity lights in reading areas, and so forth.

■ Types of Disability

In addition to people who are either born with a disability or develop a disability as a young person, a significant number of people become disabled in their most productive years from accidents, mental illness, brain or spinal cord injuries, stroke, Parkinson's, or other chronic diseases. The onset could be sudden through traumatic injury, as in the well-known case of the late Christopher Reeve, who became quadriplegic through a riding accident, or gradual, as in the case of the late comedian Richard Pryor, who experienced decreasing mobility due to multiple sclerosis.

In addition to the age-related disabilities that many of us are familiar with, either personally or through watching our aging relatives, disabilities fall into the general categories of sensory, mobility, developmental, and psychiatric. (See Figure 2.1.)

Younger individuals may have dual or multiple diagnoses. Individuals with cerebral palsy, a developmental disability caused by lack of oxygen to the brain during birth, may have difficulty walking, using their hands, or speaking clearly, and may or may not have cognitive impairments. The important point is to focus on the individual, not the disability. A developmental disability is defined as one with an onset prior to age 22 that interferes with one or more activities of daily living. Examples are cerebral palsy, autism, and learning disabilities.

■ Accommodation

The Eastern Paralyzed Veterans Association describes the Americans with Disabilities Act (ADA) as enabling people with disabilities "to participate more fully in their communities and gain more complete access to the goods and services most Americans take for granted." The word **accommodation** in connection with disability refers to the way a task or physical space is modified so that a person with a disability can participate in spite of whatever challenges the disability may pose.

Figure 2.1 | Types of Disability

CATEGORY	TYPE OF DISABILITY	LIMITATIONS
Sensory	Deafness/hard of hearing	Limits access to spoken communication.
	Blindness/impaired vision	Limits access to visual information, both pictures and printed documents such as listings, mortgage documents, and contracts.
Mobility	Mobility impairment	May necessitate a wheelchair or cane. Person can be limited by physical barriers in the environment such as steps and curbs. Environment may need modification to accommodate wheelchair.
Developmental	May include all of the above and/or cognitive issues or speech impairment.	Limitations may be similar to those experienced by persons with any of the above disabilities. There may also be learning limitations.
Psychiatric	Mental illness, including but not limited to clinical depression, schizophrenia, bipolar disorder	May affect understanding and interpersonal interactions.

Accommodation allows for **participation**, full engagement in society. In working with clients with disabilities, you will discover the need for a number of different accommodations, some of which may require some form of assistive technology.

The Individuals with Disabilities Education Act (IDEA), the federal special education law, defines an **assistive technology device** as "any item, piece of equipment, or product system … that is used to increase, maintain, or improve functional capabilities of individuals with disabilities." Handi-Ramp, a company specializing in disability and accessibility products, maintains a listing of real estate agents and brokers that specialize in supporting people with disabilities and gives contact information for agencies dealing with assistive technology in various states (*www.handi-ramp.com*).

Every community is served by an **independent living center** where you can learn more about accommodation and in some cases borrow or rent assistive devices including temporary ramps, communication boards, and TTY devices. Visit the Web site *www.virtualcil.net/cils* to find your closest independent living center.

◾ People First—Building Relationships

When looking at houses with a person who has a disability, you will need to know what the person wants and needs in terms of their surroundings, so it is perfectly appropriate to ask. And then listen. Carefully. Ask questions when you are not sure you understand. People with disabilities accept your interest in them and appreciate being asked respectfully about how to best accommodate them. If a person with mobility impairment leaves their wheelchair and crawls around the house or is carried to the basement by a parent or aide, this is how they adapt to their situation. Respect their personal accommodation to the situation. Often the limitation is imposed more by barrier in the environment than by the disability itself. People don't want to be patronized or considered heroic or brave for the manner in which they have learned to accomplish day-to-day tasks. The "Ten

Commandments of Etiquette for Communicating with People with Disabilities" (see Appendix A) has been adopted by many organizations, including Century 21 and other real estate firms.

Etiquette for Communicating with People with Disabilities

People with disabilities are entitled to the same courtesies, including personal privacy, you would extend to anyone. If you find it inappropriate to ask personal questions of your friends, extend the same courtesy to a person with a disability.

- If you don't make a habit of leaning or hanging on people, don't lean or hang on someone's wheelchair. Wheelchairs are an extension of personal space.

- When you offer to assist someone with vision impairment, allow the person to take your arm. This will help you to guide, rather than propel or lead, the person.

- Treat adults as adults. Use a person's first name only when you extend this familiarity to everyone present. Don't patronize people who use wheelchairs by patting them on the head or shoulder. Reserve this sign of affection for children.

- In conversation with someone who has a disability, speak directly to him or her, rather than through a companion who may be present.

- Relax. Don't be embarrassed if you happen to use common expressions, such as "See you later" or "I've got to run," that seem to relate to the person's disability.

- To get the attention of a person who has a hearing impairment, tap the person on the shoulder or wave your hand. Look directly at the person and speak clearly, slowly, and expressively to establish if the person can read your lips. Not everyone with hearing impairments can lip-read. Those who do will rely on facial expressions and other body language to help understand. Show consideration by facing a light source and keeping your hands and food away from your mouth when speaking. Keep mustaches well trimmed. Written notes will help, but talking louder will not.

- When talking with a person in a wheelchair for more than a few minutes, place yourself at the wheelchair user's eye level to spare both of you a stiff neck.

- When greeting a person with a severe loss of vision, always identify yourself and others who may be with you. Say, for example, "To your left is Jim Bailer." When conversing in a group, remember to say the name of the person to whom you are speaking to give a vocal cue. Speak in a normal tone of voice, indicate when you move from one place to another, and let it be known when the conversation is at an end.

- When talking to a person who has difficulty speaking, give whole, unhurried attention. Keep your manner encouraging, and be patient rather than feel you should speak for the person. When necessary, ask questions that require short answers or a nod or shake of the head. Never pretend to understand if you are having difficulty doing so. Repeat what you understand. The person's reaction will guide you to understanding.

- It all comes down to common courtesy:
  - If you would like to help someone with a disability, ask if he or she needs it before you act, and listen to any instructions the person may want to give.
  - When giving directions to a person in a wheelchair, consider distance, weather conditions, and physical obstacles such as stairs, curbs, and steep hills.

- When directing a person with a visual impairment, use specifics such as "left a hundred feet" or "right about two yards"
- Be considerate of the extra time it might take a person with a disability to get things done or said. Let the person set the pace in walking and talking.
- When planning events involving persons with disabilities, consider their needs beforehand. If an inaccessible barrier exists, let them know about it prior to the event.

■ People First—Language

People with disabilities have historically been defined by their medical diagnosis and talked about as if they constituted a nondiverse, monolithic group chiefly characterized by the limitations associated with their condition. Recognizing that language can perpetuate these stereotypes, the disability community advocates for the use of **people first language.** (See Figure 2.2.)

Figure 2.2 | Examples of People First Language

You should say:	Instead of:
People with disabilities	The handicapped or disabled
Paul has a cognitive disability (diagnosis)	He's mentally retarded
Kate has autism (or a diagnosis of …)	She's autistic
Ryan has Down syndrome (or a diagnosis of …)	He's Down's; a Down's person; mongoloid
Sara has a learning disability (diagnosis)	She's learning disabled
Bob has a physical disability (diagnosis)	He's a quadriplegic/is crippled
Mary is of short stature/she's a little person	She's a dwarf/midget
Tom has a mental health condition	He's emotionally disturbed/mentally ill
Nora uses a wheelchair/mobility chair	She's confined to/is wheelchair bound
Steve receives special ed services	He's in special ed; he's a sped student
Tonya has a developmental delay	She's developmentally delayed
Children without disabilities	Normal/healthy/typical children
Communicates with her eyes/device/etc.	Is nonverbal
Customer	Client, consumer, recipient, etc.
Congenital disability	Birth defect
Brain injury	Brain damaged
Accessible parking, hotel room, etc.	Handicapped parking, hotel room, etc.
She needs … or she uses …	She has problems/special needs

■ Practical Considerations

Heeding several practical considerations and tips can make relationships more satisfying for both you and potential homebuyers who have disabilities.

Communication

Depending upon the person's disability you may need an interpreter, a family member present, a sharp listening ear, or some other accommodation. Most important, be patient, listen carefully, and ask questions. For people who are deaf, a telephone relay system is available to assist in phone communication. By dialing 711 an operator can assist you with communications with deaf and hard of hearing people.

Learn how to use the relay for the deaf and hard of hearing by contacting your local resource agency. And if your office gets a call from someone who is hard to understand, take it seriously and never assume the call is a joke. It is most likely a person with a speech impairment who is communicating as best as he or she can, and who expects the same service and respect as your other clients.

People with intellectual disabilities, traumatic brain injuries or other neurological impairments, and those who have had strokes will need special accommodation to understand what you are trying to communicate. Again, you may have to explain something several times or simplify your remarks. You may have to communicate with family members, support staff, trustees, or guardians instead of communicating with the individual that will be living in the home, but be careful to direct your remarks to the client rather than talking about him or her in the third person. In some situations you will be working with someone who communicates with a communication board or a computer assisted system.

Travel and Mobility

Many people with disabilities have their own transportation in the form of accessible vans or cars or access to para-transit buses or accessible city buses. Some of your clients may need you to drive them to see a home. They will tell you how to help them transfer into your car and how to fold and store their wheelchair in your car. Be very careful with their chair. It is their primary source of mobility and an essential part of their life. Doing what is reasonable to assist the customer is required by law and should be your goal.

Interpreters

If you are working with someone who is hearing impaired, you may need to use the services of a sign language interpreter to assist with communication. Contact your local independent living center to secure interpreter services if the client cannot bring an interpreter. Look in the yellow pages for translators and interpreters or ask your client how to arrange for interpreter services. Under Title III of the Americans with Disabilities Act you are responsible to pay for the interpreter services. There is a growing pool of real estate licensees who know sign language. Coldwell Banker has been active in offering a sign language service to prospective buyers.

Using the Telephone Relay

The telephone relay allows people who are deaf or hearing impaired to communicate via telephone. The relay is accessed by dialing 711. You or the client can dial 711 to access an operator that has access to a TTY machine. The client types their message on their TTY and the operator reads the message to you. You then respond by talking through the operator to your client. The operator types your response to your client. Your conversation is with the potential purchaser and not the operator. If your office gets a call from the operator saying there is a call from the "relay" you will know that a person who is hearing-impaired is trying to reach your office.

■ Don't Assume, Just Ask

While it is illegal under fair housing laws to ask about whether or not a client has a disability or ask for details unless the person raises the issue, once you have established a relationship with the possible buyer you should ask if you are not clear about what accommodations are needed or how to communicate. People with disabilities are always willing to tell others how to help them. It is part of their life and part of having a disability. They appreciate you asking instead of assuming. They know best how to satisfy their needs for communication, mobility, and understanding, so feel comfortable about asking.

■ Decision Making: The People Around the Person

In many cases, you will be working with more than one individual. It may be a couple, two friends, or parent and child. Sometimes when working with a person with a cognitive or intellectual disability, you may be working with the individual, their parents, support staff or personal assistants, a guardian, and/or a trustee. We will explore these relationships.

The Individual

You are familiar with working with individuals. You provide good client service, and work within their budget and their wishes. You help make the deal that is the best for your client. It is the same when working with a person with a disability. You may have to learn a few new things about various sources of income, and learn different ways to communicate with and support the customer. You will learn about what it means to have a disability and the specifics of different types of disabilities as you serve this client base.

Families

Working with families of clients is not uncommon. Parents want to be involved and assist in the purchase process of their child's home. You no doubt have experience working with families. Parents of children with disabilities have a much more challenging role and can be very protective of things they perceive as a threat to their child. While they want a normal life for their child, they sometimes are afraid of letting go, and subsequently can be somewhat negative during the process. It is important that the family is comfortable with the home and the transaction.

Support Staff

Some individuals with disabilities will have support staff (case managers, social workers, and/or personal care assistants) assist them in visiting houses and arranging the financing. This is a different situation than what you face in most transactions and it can be more time consuming. Sometimes the support staff can also be very protective. There can be conflict if the support staff and the family are not on the same page.

Personal Care Assistants

You may find yourself communicating not only with the client, but the family, assistant, and case manager. People with disabilities often hire aides or personal assistants/attendants to help them with the activities of daily living such as eating, transferring, toileting, dressing, etc. If your client has an established relationship with an assistant or caregiver, that person may very well accompany the person with a disability when they look at homes. Assistants are experienced in navigating accessibility barriers and may also be helpful in communication since they are accustomed to understanding and meeting their clients' needs. For instance, if you have difficulty understanding your client's speech after several repetitions, it is appropriate to say, "I'm sorry, I still don't understand; do you think your aide could help me?" The assistant can then either clarify what was said or help you use a communication board or other device. In some cases, the assistant may carry the person with a disability, or otherwise physically assist in ways you are not accustomed to seeing. The point is to relax, knowing that these two people are used to each other and have worked out these accommodations over time, and to be respectful of the means they've developed. Note that there can sometimes be conflict between the person with a disability and his family or assistants, and agents should actively avoid getting caught in the middle.

Guardians

Some persons with severe intellectual disabilities and other cognitive disorders are not competent to make decisions. In these situations, a **court-appointed guardian** assumes the role of decision maker for the individual. The court permits guardians, depending upon the severity of the disability, to have total or partial decision making for the individual. Generally, parents, siblings, or other relatives are the guardians, but there may be nonrelative guardians appointed. Guardian decision making powers may be granted over some or all financial, legal, medical, services, and other matters.

Working with a guardian is like working with a parent of a dependent child. The guardian has the legal authority to enter into contracts and to make financial and medical decisions. A guardian generally has the best interests of the individual in mind.

Trustees

When a special or supplemental needs trust (see Chapter 3) is established for an individual with a disability, a **trustee** is appointed to manage the funds, report to appropriate government agencies, pay taxes on earnings, and pay eligible expenses for the beneficiary of the trust. In some transactions the client will have a special needs trust to assist in the payment of their expenses. In other situations, the trust may be the owner of the property, so the trustee will be the client along with the individual with the disability.

The transaction may be more time consuming with the additional people involved. Working with additional parties may be confusing at first, but all of the parties have the same goal: a home for the person with the disability.

Industry Profile: Serving the Community

Paula Gaies
Weichert REALTORS® Northeast Group
Albany, NY

I believe that when you work in the community, when you take money from the community, you have to give back through community service. Working with people with disabilities has given me the opportunity to do just that—to do something related to my industry, using the skills I already have, to serve people with special challenges.

At the beginning, I knew that we needed some specific knowledge about accessibility and finance opportunities, but more than anything, I viewed my first transaction as a leap of faith.

But do you know who helped me the most? The people I thought I was serving. They helped me feel comfortable with them, with their needs. Their enthusiasm and determination were what made me stick with whatever challenges we had along the way.

One client who used a wheelchair wished to see the basement of a home she was being shown, and she asked her aide to carry her down the steps. "She must feel embarrassed that I am seeing her so vulnerable," I thought. Yet, she accomplished what she wanted to do: surveyed the entire home, bought the home, and everyone moved on. It was a triumph for her to accomplish what she set out to do.

Following another sale, the client invited me to his housewarming. His whole family—cousins, aunts and uncles, brothers and sisters, mother and father were there, and everyone expressed their deep gratitude, telling me in their own way what a difference this purchase would make in my client's life. The extra effort and planning I had put in was all worthwhile when I saw just how much this home meant to him and his family.

It may seem like there are more layers of responsibility in such a transaction than in a traditional real estate sale. On the agent end, you have to have a buyer who is going to be flexible. Everyone has to have an open mind, and the client with a disability needs a very supportive family, particularly if they are involved with the purchase.

I usually encourage, almost demand, that the primary caregiver come to see the house with the client. So, rather than just take the client out, I took the client, his mother, his aunt, and other relatives or friends, if desired—it made for some logistical planning, but we didn't have to duplicate our efforts. We all did it together and were on the same page from the outset.

Last year, I won an award for handling a single transaction that made a difference in the community. The client was a young man with disabilities, and we were successful in arranging a Home of Your Own mortgage and additional grants. At the end, he was able to afford a home well over what he originally thought possible.

When accepting the award before a group of 300 agents, I said, "Yes, this transaction was hard, but it made me feel good and let me know I was doing good. I challenged the audience to work a little harder, move a little outside their comfort zone, and learn about serving this market—the challenges, the opportunities, the joys."

■ Chapter 2 Review Questions

1. The ADA defines a disability as a
   a. life altering disability that anyone acquires during his or her lifetime.
   b. physical or mental impairment that substantially limits a major life activity.
   c. spinal cord injury.
   d. mental illness.

2. Proper etiquette when dealing with persons of various disabilities includes
   a. using the disability name when addressing the person.
   b. asking what type of assistance the person needs or will need.
   c. only talking to the guardian about the needs of the person.
   d. meeting the person in a public place first.

3. The decision maker(s) for a person with a severe disability can be the
   a. trustee.
   b. parents.
   c. guardian(s).
   d. All of the above

4. When showing a house to a person who is blind you should
   a. offer your arm to guide him or her around the house.
   b. take his or her arm and lead the individual around the home.
   c. tell him or her to go left or right as they walk around the room.
   d. do nothing, as the individual probably will need no help.

5. Which of the following is a resource to help you communicate directly with a client with disabilities?
   a. 711 relay for the deaf and sign language interpreters
   b. Disability law attorneys
   c. Mortgage brokers
   d. Other real estate professionals

6. A developmental disability
   a. is a mental illness.
   b. always results from a traumatic brain injury.
   c. occurs as part of the aging process.
   d. is a lifelong disability that occurs before the age of 22.

7. If a person is in a wheelchair you should
   a. place yourself at their eye level.
   b. frequently touch their wheelchair.
   c. pat them on the head when they leave.
   d. speak loudly.

8. All of the following are acceptable examples of people first language *EXCEPT*
   a. Bob has a mental health condition.
   b. Maria uses a mobility chair.
   c. Josh has a diagnosis of Down syndrome.
   d. Lee is developmentally delayed.

9. A guardian is
   a. someone who protects a person with a disability.
   b. a member of a support group for persons with disabilities.
   c. a court-appointed person or organization that provides decision making services for a person not capable of decision making.
   d. a parent or other relative.

10. What is a trustee's role in relationship to an individual with a disability?
   a. to manage funds and pay bills for the beneficiary.
   b. to save money in the trust for the persons that receive the remainder of the trust.
   c. to speak on behalf of the beneficiary.
   d. to make sure the beneficiary's siblings are taken care of with trust proceeds.

Financing Sources

Learning Objectives

After completing this chapter, you will be able to

- List income streams a buyer with disabilities might have

- Describe a blending of financing sources that could qualify a buyer

- Explain how you might work with an agency representative payee

- Locate funding sources for accessibility modifications

- Identify sources of funding that can be applied to homeownership, including down payment assistance

■ Key Terms

Community Development Block Grant (CDBG)	individual development account (IDA)	Small Cities Block Grant (SCBG)
Community Reinvestment Act (CRA)	Low-Income Housing Tax Credit (LIHTC)	Social Security Disability Insurance (SSDI)
Federal Home Loan Bank (FHLB)	Medicaid	supplemental needs trust (SNT)
Home Investment Partnership Program (HOME)	Rural Development Services (RDS)	Supplemental Security Income (SSI)
	Section 8 program	

In this chapter, you will become familiar with the common forms of income and types of assets and credit that people with disabilities may have, as well as special resources they can use to qualify for mortgages. You will also learn more about guardianship, special needs trusts, and working with agencies.

■ Assets and Income

As with any client, you need to start with the mortgage range the client qualifies for in order to show appropriate properties. This section will help you to gain a sense of the types of income, credit, and other assets people with disabilities may have for down payment and closing costs, as well as programs targeted to homeownership for people with disabilities. In familiarizing yourself with benefits, you can ensure the potential homeowner is bringing all the income and assets he or she is eligible for to the home purchase.

While many people with disabilities derive their income from employment, many receive their income from entitlement programs. These programs have asset limitations that have ramifications for home purchase—people requiring medical assistance such as Medicaid, or who anticipate not being able to work because of their disability, increasingly use financial vehicles such as special needs trusts.

■ Income Sources

Employment Income

Employment income is the type of income you are most familiar with in working with clients. This source of income may be from a regular job or from some type of sheltered or supported employment program for persons with disabilities.

Supplemental Security Income

Supplemental Security Income (SSI) is a benefit for persons who have been disabled for most of their life, do not have a work history, and are generally not able to work. A person born with an intellectual disability or a severe physical disability would be likely to receive SSI. SSI was designed to pay for food, shelter, and clothing expenses for the individual. The person with a disability, or a person representing him or her (representative payee), receives the SSI benefit monthly. The SSI monthly benefit is adjusted annually for inflation. The 2007 SSI benefit is $623 for an eligible individual and $934 for an eligible couple. Some states supplement SSI benefits to increase the monthly payment and the amount varies by state.

Social Security Disability Insurance

Social Security Disability Insurance (SSDI) provides monthly income for a person who becomes disabled after they have a work history. A number of persons become disabled during their work years from disease, illness, or accidents. SSDI is a social security insurance program that allows one to continue to receive income. Monthly amounts depend upon one's earnings, but an average monthly payment for someone making $40,000 per year is approximately $1,300 per month. Spouses and children can also receive benefits under this program. For more details and information on SSDI, see the following Web sites: *www.ssa.gov/disability* and *www.ssa.gov/planners/index.htm.*

Medicaid

Medicaid is a program jointly funded by federal, state, and local governments to meet the medical and long-term care services for persons with low incomes and long-term disabilities. Long-term care services are provided for persons with disabilities needing medical transportation, personal care services, and other services to help them live in the community. All states have Medicaid waiver services to assist persons with disabilities to live more independently, rather than a more expensive institution. Medicaid waiver services can include funds for case management, accessibility modifications, in-home personal assistance, day program services, transportation, live-in caregivers, and other services depending upon the state and targeted population of the individual state's waiver.

Medicaid eligibility is a plus in qualifying a person for a mortgage due to the health and long-term care expense coverage. Waiver services are usually individualized to meet the needs of the beneficiary and in some states the waiver offers coverage for the room and board expenses of the live-in caregiver. This coverage can be applied to homeownership in that Medicaid will pay for the percentage of the home which the live-in companion uses and shares and therefore should be factored in when determining the purchaser's income. For example, if a person buys a three-bedroom home, Medicaid coverage for the live-in caregiver pays for one third of the expenses of the home. This added Medicaid income is important to consider when qualifying the potential purchaser.

Family Income and Resources

Family income and resources include any assistance that parents or other relatives of a person with a disability make available for the housing and living expenses of the individual. This may include down payment and closing cost assistance, assistance with monthly payments, providing some or all of the maintenance needs, and other needs. This income and assistance may be partial, total, one time, or ongoing. Each situation will be different. Upon the death of the individual's parents, ongoing assistance may come from a special or supplemental needs trust.

Special or Supplemental Needs Trust

A special or **supplemental needs trust (SNT)** is a legal, financial tool created for the benefit of the person with a disability to supplement government benefits and entitlements. A special needs trust is managed by a third party, the trustee. It allows a person with a disability to have assets to pay for goods and services not paid for by government disability benefit programs. An SNT can own property, dispose of property, and own a variety of investments. Regular payouts from a trust can be used in qualifying an individual for a mortgage.

The assets of the trust can come from parents, grandparents, or others, and can be transferred directly into a third party SNT or can come directly to the person with a disability from a court settlement or gift into a first party trust. The trust may cover all homeownership expenses, a portion of the housing costs, or it may just supplement some of the client's expenses.

SNTs are regulated by state and federal law and regulation under the Social Security Administration and local Medicaid agencies. Trust income pays for things that are not covered by government benefits. Social Security's Supplemental Security Income (SSI) pays for food, shelter, and clothing. The trust can supplement those payments and cover utilities and home maintenance. However, if the trust pays for food, shelter, or clothing costs, the amount of SSI a person receives may be reduced.

Increasingly, SNTs are being used to help family members purchase homes. Sometimes a group of parents will set up a third party trust in order to purchase homes for their adult children. There are various ways this can be done. The trust may own the home and cover all principal, interest, taxes, insurance, and maintenance costs, or it may rent the home to the beneficiary of the trust. The trust may also charge beneficiaries for certain expenses related to their housing costs.

If a client has a trust that will be used to assist in paying housing expenses, you may find yourself working with the trustee in the purchase and prequalification process. If the person with a disability has a guardian and trustee (they can be the same person), you will find that they can be major decision makers in the home-buying process. The trust attorney who established the trust may also be involved to safeguard the interests of the trust and their client's ongoing eligibility for government benefits.

Other Income

Roommates are also important in sharing living expenses. Most married couples, friends, and recent graduates share their living expenses to keep their budgets under control. Likewise, persons with disabilities may have roommates as co-purchasers, renters, or as live-in staff. This additional income can be calculated in determining total income when working with a client.

■ Savings Programs, Down Payment, Closing Costs, and Rehabilitation Assistance

Often people with disabilities will accumulate funds for down payment and closing costs the traditional way, by saving. However, individuals who receive their income from benefits such as SSI and SSDI face special challenges. These programs come with stringent asset limitations. People receiving these benefits often cannot earn more than a certain amount through employment and cannot accumulate enough savings for a down payment without jeopardizing their benefits. The asset limitations are part of the reason special needs trusts are set up. These trusts allow individuals to own a home while continuing to be eligible for SSI and Medicaid.

Homeownership is a dream for many Americans, and the Federal Government has supported programs that enhance homeownership. Following is a list of a number of programs that people with disabilities have accessed to help with homeownership. Getting to know the agencies in your area that administer these programs (including the local area agencies serving people with disabilities) gives you valuable information and can help you target this market.

Individual Development Accounts

An **individual development account (IDA)** is a matched savings account that community-based organizations, including the local area agencies that support people with disabilities, are increasingly using to help low-income people build assets to use toward homeownership, higher education, or small business ownership. First established under the Personal Responsibility and Work Opportunity Reconciliation Act of 1996 (commonly referred to as welfare reform), IDAs encourage savings by offering low-income persons 1:1, 2:1, or more generous matches for their own regular deposits. These matched savings accounts are similar to 401(k) plans and other matched savings accounts, but can serve a broad range of purposes.

IDA programs are implemented by community-based organizations in partnership with a financial institution that holds the deposits, and are funded by public and private sources. Federal and state governments and/or private sector organizations and individuals can match deposits for low-income families, and many IDA programs include financial literacy training and counseling in financial planning. Financial institutions, including community banks and credit unions, are currently running IDA programs, and many other financial institutions are funding IDA programs and holding accounts. There are over 500 IDA initiatives across the country and at least 10,000 people are currently saving in IDAs. For more information on state-by-state policy on IDAs and funding sources, see the

Web site *http://gwbweb.wustl.edu/csd/Policy/StateIDAtableRevised2007.pdf*. If you know your client receives service from a local area agency, you can ask if they have an IDA program when discussing down payment options.

Home Investment Partnership Program

The **Home Investment Partnership Program (HOME)** can pay for down payment and closing costs and/or moderate rehabilitation (remodeling) for first time home-buyers. Up to $22,500 can be given to new homebuyers in the form of a forgivable loan. If the person stays in the home for the required number of years, the loan is forgiven. If the buyer sells during the regulatory period, they have to pay back a prorated share of the loan. Money flows from the U.S. Department of Housing and Urban Development to states and municipalities. The states in turn either admin-ister the funds themselves or give grants to local nonprofit housing agencies to work with the homebuyers.

To find out who in your area administers these funds, contact your municipal government's housing or community development office, your county planning or community development office, or your state housing agencies. They will help identify where and when these funds are available.

Because these funds are predicated on the federal budget cycle, they are not always available. The process of qualifying for the funds may either be on a first come, first served basis or by lottery. Some states award HOME funds to organizations that serve persons with disabilities. All administering agency and nonprofit HOME recipients are required by Section 504 of HUD regulation to set aside 7 percent of the funds for persons with disabilities. For more information on this program, see the Web site *www.hud.gov/groups/disabilities.cfm*.

Block Grants

Community Development Block Grant/Small Cities Block Grant (CDBG/SCBG) programs can be used to assist homeowners to purchase, remodel, and maintain their homes. These federal funds from HUD are a yearly allocation to states and municipalities for many local needs. Eligible projects include community policing, park maintenance, curb cuts, paving, and building new town facilities. The block grants can also be used for down payment and closing costs assistance, moderate remodeling for new owners, and maintenance for existing low- and moderate-income homeowners. As a real estate salesperson or broker, you should be aware of these funds to assist low- and moderate-income purchasers in your municipal-ity. These funds often show up in the form of city- or county-based down payment assistance programs. You can obtain more information from your city or county Web site, if that locale has chosen to develop a down payment assistance program. It should also be noted that most of these funds are limited to first time home-buyers. Consider asking staff from the municipality to address one of your staff meetings so you and colleagues are current on the programs available.

Low Income Housing Tax Credit

The **Low Income Housing Tax Credit (LIHTC)** is a vehicle by which individuals with disabilities can lease a property for a 12- to 30-year period and, at the end of that period, have an opportunity to buy the property. This is a complex transac-tion but does represent a financing opportunity that realtors and their prospective clients can learn more about by contacting their state housing agency or a bank.

Federal Home Loan Bank

The **Federal Home Loan Bank (FHLB)** has several programs to assist homebuyers.

- Through the Affordable Housing Program, the FHLB give grants to member banks to use as down payment and closing costs, buydown of interest rates and principal, or for moderate remodeling. Member banks have developed various programs through the Affordable Housing Program. One example is the Federal Home Loan Bank of New York's First Home Club, a special set-aside available to first time homeowners through participating member lenders. The New York FHL bank provides down payment and closing cost assistance by granting up to $3 in matching funds for each dollar saved to households who participate in an approved homeownership counseling program and follow a systematic savings plan. Up to $5,000 of matching funds can be awarded to qualifying households based on the total savings deposited in a First Home Club savings account. For more information, see the Web site *www.fhlbanks.com.*

- The Community Investment Program provides below market rate loans to assist member banks to extend long term financing to low- and moderate-income individuals. The interest rate on these mortgages can be as low as 1 percent. See the FHLB's Web site for more information: *www.fhlbanks.com/ html/programs.html*

Some states and municipalities have additional programs for down payment and other forms of assistance related to homeownership. In California, for instance, the California Homebuyers Down Payment Assistance Program provides assistance in the form of second loans for down payment and closing costs (*www.calhfa.ca.gov/homeownership/programs/chdap.htm*). As mentioned in Chapter 1, the Milwaukee area has IndependenceFirst, a comprehensive homeownership program for people with disabilities (*www.independencefirst.org/services/other/ home_ownership.asp*).

■ Mortgage Products

The **Rural Development Services (RDS)** of the United States Department of Agriculture has a number of programs that can assist homeowners, including low-interest mortgages and moderate remodeling loans and grants. Having a speaker from RDS at a staff meeting can make your office aware of programs that you can use in working with persons with disabilities or low- and moderate-income clients. By going to their Web site, *www.rurdev.usda.gov,* you can access information on U.S. Department of Agriculture mortgages, grants, and loan programs and the locations of their local offices.

Fannie Mae

Fannie Mae partnered with the National Home of Your Own Alliance to develop a mortgage product that meets the needs of persons with disabilities. As a result of this partnership, the Home Choice™ mortgage (which later became Community HomeChoice™) was designed for persons with disabilities and their families. The basic Community HomeChoice™ mortgage has the following features:

- 100% financing is available.
- Coalitions provide grants and other assistance to help borrowers with down payment and closing costs, access modifications, and property repairs, and provide budget management and support services that include homeownership education counseling.

- A co-borrower who will not be living in the home may be part of the transaction, as long as the co-borrower is a family member or legal guardian. (For example, a parent could sign the mortgage with a child, even if the parent does not plan to live in the home.) However, this varies from state to state.

- Eligible borrowers include any low- or moderate-income person defined as disabled by the Americans with Disabilities Act of 1990 or defined as handicapped by the Fair Housing Amendments Act of 1988. Family members living in the home may be co-borrowers.

- Owner-occupied single-family detached homes, townhouses, and condominiums are eligible.

For more information go to *www.fanniemae.com* and click on "Find a Mortgage."

Note that there are some differences among states. California, for example, has piggybacked state funds to allow the Community HomeChoice™ loan to be offered at even lower interest rates—a fixed 3 percent, 30-year mortgage. Also, California does not allow for non-occupant co-borrowers, unlike the generic version of Community HomeChoice™. Other states providing special financing may also have this restriction. Community HomeChoice mortgage products in many states have been modified as a result of partnerships with state housing finance agencies. Check with your state Fannie Mae Partnership office for the particulars in your state.

Community Reinvestment Act (CRA)

The **Community Reinvestment Act (CRA)** is a federal law that requires banks offering services in a neighborhood to make mortgages available to it customers. Most banks have CRA officers or departments to ensure they meet federal requirements for investing in their service areas. Working with the CRA staff of the banks in your area can help establish a number of activities for your customers, such as funding individual development accounts, homebuyer training programs, specialized mortgage products, and underwriting criteria for persons with disabilities. Time spent with CRA staff can result in collaborations and products that will increase your effectiveness in delivering services to lower-income people.

■ State and Local Programs

To find out about programs that may be available in your state, contact your state's Housing Finance Agency. See the National Council of State Housing Agencies to locate the agency in your state, *www.ncsha.org/section.cfm/4/39/187.*

Section 8

The **Section 8 program** has traditionally been seen as a rental assistance program, but in 2000, rules were changed allowing recipients to use Section 8 to become homeowners; thus, many administrators of Section 8 now fund homeownership. The rental assistance program works through federally funded, local housing authorities (of which there are many throughout the U.S.). It subsidizes the renter's payment by paying the landlord the bulk of the monthly rent.

Where Section 8 housing programs exist, borrowers may qualify to have their monthly payment and their subsidy from the housing authority applied toward a mortgage payment to a bank instead of toward a rent payment to the Section 8 landlord. You need to be knowledgeable about the programs in your area. You may want to start by contacting your local housing authority. Blending these various income streams can help to qualify low-income clients for mortgages they can afford.

Telephone Lifeline and Energy Assistance

The Telephone Lifeline Program (TLP) is offered on a state-by-state basis. The Lifeline Program provides financial assistance to low-income residents to help ensure that those customers can afford basic telephone services. The programs provide discounts when establishing service, lower monthly service charges, and special payment arrangements.

Energy assistance is available at the state level through the U.S. Department of Health and Human Services Low Income Energy Assistance Program (LHEAP).

Tax Abatement Programs

Many counties and municipalities have tax abatement programs for persons on fixed incomes, seniors, veterans, and persons with disabilities. Your knowledge of these municipalities and their tax policies can be critical in the qualification process. If a person qualifies for a 15 percent tax abatement in one municipality and not another, your knowledge will be invaluable to your customer.

Other Local Programs

In addition to the private, federal, and state funds discussed, organizations such as Habitat for Humanity, local foundations and endowments, banks, businesses, religious social organizations, and some real estate industry–sponsored housing opportunity foundations have grant and loan programs to assist persons with disabilities achieve their homeownership goals. Such opportunities should not be overlooked.

■ Working Locally with an Agency

Many agencies serving persons with disabilities have funds to assist with housing expenses, utilities, food, case management services, homemaker services, personal care aides, and other supports that help one live independently. Some municipalities have tax abatement programs for seniors, persons with disabilities, and veterans to reduce their property tax.

Agency staff can play a role helping people buy a house. Caseworkers may accompany people to look at houses and assist them with answering questions, interpreting responses, completing mortgage applications, and building bridges between the potential buyer and the real estate agent. Some agencies may help with down payment or closing costs. Further, some people's service needs are paid for through Medicaid, a portion of which can be allocated to housing costs in cases where the person requires overnight or live-in care. This option is for a live-in companion whose room and board costs are paid by Medicaid. It can be used in calculating income when developing a budget for the individual.

Service provider agencies are becoming more actively involved in purchasing homes with or for their clients because they are mandated by a number of laws, regulations, and court cases to develop and provide housing in the least restrictive setting. Sometimes an agency, family member, or friend will act as your client's representative payee. A representative payee takes on paying the person's bills, including the mortgage payment. A representative payee is appointed by the Social Security Administration for persons not able to make appropriate decisions. To find out what agencies are available to people with disabilities in your state, see *www.nichcy.org/states.htm*.

■ Prequalifying a Client with Disabilities

Activities of the National Home of Your Own Alliance helped develop the concept of budget-based qualifying for a mortgage. This concept looks at the total of all sources of income from families, benefits, entitlements, employment income, trust income, down payment and closing cost assistance programs, and services to determine qualification for a mortgage if there is not enough regular employment income to qualify in a traditional way.

This process of blending a variety of funding sources and identification of how a person presently pays their living expenses with existing public and private benefits, gives you and the financial institution a different way to look at a person's income. Also remember that many of these benefits are not taxable and the income can be grossed up.

Many of the finance agencies in states involved in the National Home of Your Own Alliance changed underwriting criteria to assist in qualifying persons with disabilities. For example, the State of New York Mortgage Agency developed a Home of Your Own 30-year mortgage, with a 4 percent fixed interest rate and no down payment or closing costs.

The following example describes how budget-based qualifying was used to determine one applicant's income.

Kathy had a skiing accident that resulted in both physical and cognitive disabilities. Due to this accident, Kathy is not able to work full-time and requires assistance with her daily activities.

She receives Social Security Disability Insurance, food stamps, heating assistance, Telephone Lifeline, trust income, and room and board income from a live in-caregiver. Kathy's monthly income is predictable, given her income sources, and the income is expected to continue for the rest of her life. At times she has some employment income from part-time employment, but that income is not predictable.

As can be seen in this example, Kathy's income is based more upon budget-based revenue sources than an income-based situation. If Kathy were to apply for a mortgage, all of the sources discussed would be taken into consideration to determine her actual total income.

■ Funds for Accessibility Modifications

Many of the programs and organizations previously mentioned can be used to fund accessibility modification to one's home. The State of Minnesota's Housing Finance Agency has a comprehensive list of funding sources that can be accessed at their Web site: *www.mhfa.state.mn.us/homes/Access_Financing_Grid.pdf*.

The Illinois-based company Handi-Ramp developed a Home Access program that real estate professionals can join to

■ provide additional services to those with a need for accessible housing;

■ network with potential clients as well as other consultants;

■ become a specialist in providing ADA accessible housing; and

■ access a Personal ADA Advisor through Handi-Ramp.

See *www.homeaccessprogram.org* for more information.

Contact your state's vocational rehabilitation offices, developmental disability services, department of health, and local social services offices to identify sources of funding for accessibility modifications.

■ Summary

Working with a person with a disability is rewarding and challenging. As you work in this area, you will become knowledgeable about funding and mortgage products and resources available in your community. By building a good reputation with people with disabilities, their families, and service provider agencies,

Figure 3.1 | Financing Pyramid: Resources to Help with Homeownership

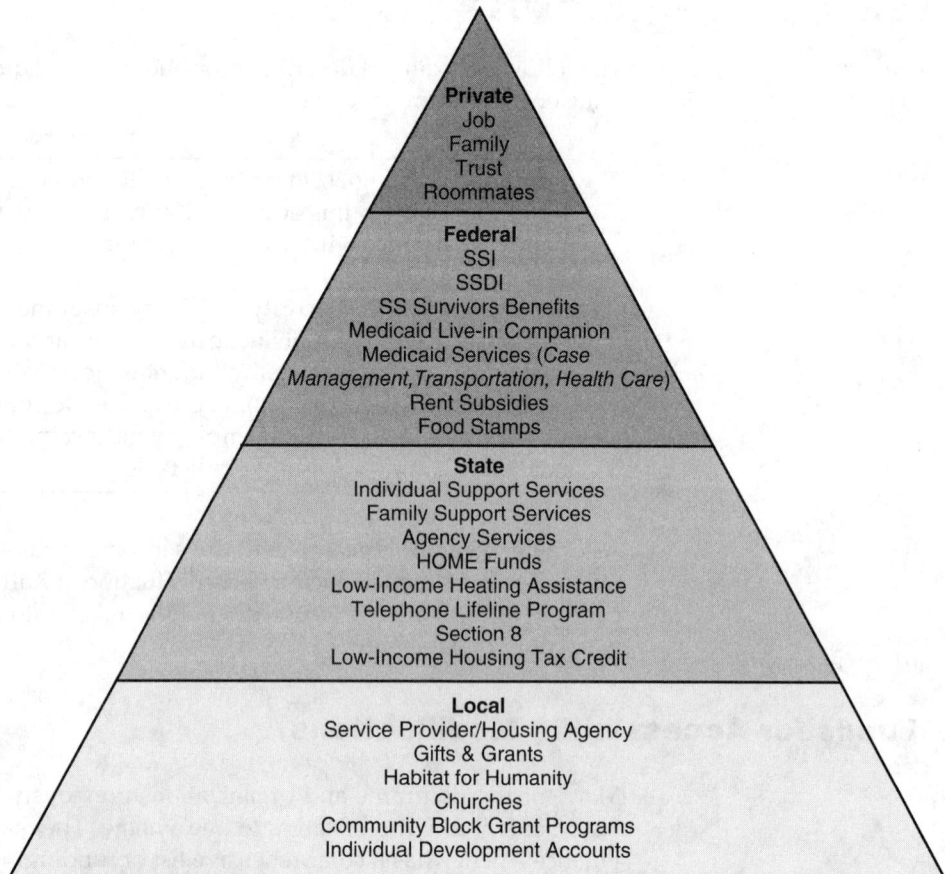

Private
Job
Family
Trust
Roommates

Federal
SSI
SSDI
SS Survivors Benefits
Medicaid Live-in Companion
Medicaid Services (*Case Management, Transportation, Health Care*)
Rent Subsidies
Food Stamps

State
Individual Support Services
Family Support Services
Agency Services
HOME Funds
Low-Income Heating Assistance
Telephone Lifeline Program
Section 8
Low-Income Housing Tax Credit

Local
Service Provider/Housing Agency
Gifts & Grants
Habitat for Humanity
Churches
Community Block Grant Programs
Individual Development Accounts

you will form relationships with families, relatives, friends, and agencies interested in purchasing homes either directly or through special trusts, thus increasing your business.

Further, by embracing this market and better understanding the various funding sources, real estate professionals are expanding another market, that of potential first-time buyers who require affordable housing.

Another way of viewing resources is in terms of private, federal, state, and local opportunities, as reflected in Figure 3.1. There is some overlap of these programs, as many are federal programs that are administered by state and local entities. Most people will know about the funds locally. In many cases, funding from these sources is blended to make the new home affordable.

■ Chapter 3 Review Questions

1. Income streams for a buyer with disabilities are *NOT* likely to include
   a. employment wages.
   b. individual development accounts.
   c. HomeChoice™ Mortgage products.
   d. Red Cross emergency relief.

2. What is an individual development account?
   a. A savings account for personal improvement courses and programs
   b. A matched savings program for homeownership and education
   c. An accounting of one's growth and improvement
   d. A personal journal of recovering milestones

3. Which of the following are funding sources for accessibility modifications?
   a. Medicaid waiver programs
   b. HOME grants and state vocational rehabilitation services
   c. Fannie Mae community mortgage products
   d. All of the above

4. Some typical blending of financing sources that could qualify a buyer with a disability include
   a. Fannie Mae HomeChoice™, Community Development Block Grants, and Supplemental Security Income.
   b. Heating Assistance Program, Telephone Lifeline, and food stamps.
   c. Section 8 rent subsidy, and emergency repair programs.
   d. State Plan Medicaid, personal care aides, and home health care aides.

5. What is Section 8?
   a. It is a term dealing with military justice and is not used for homeownership.
   b. It is a federally funded and locally administered source of rental subsidies and cannot be used for ownership payments.
   c. It is a federally funded and locally administered source of rental subsidies that can be used for mortgage payments.
   d. It is a program available only for rent subsidies.

6. Which of the following is a housing solution for one or more persons with disabilities?
   a. A family purchases a house for their child with a disability
   b. A group of families purchases a home for their children
   c. A group of individuals with disabilities pools their resources and purchases a home
   d. All of the above

7. What is a representative payee?
   a. An individual or agency appointed by Social Security to act on behalf of the person with a disability to handle their financial matters
   b. A person that is paid by Social Security to represent a person in court
   c. An individual appointed by the family to distribute funds to the person with disabilities
   d. A guardian

8. A trust can be used to help pay for
   a. rent subsidy.
   b. a mortgage.
   c. home maintenance.
   d. All of the above

9. Which of the following programs fund down payment and closing costs?
   a. HOME, CDBG, and IDAs
   b. SSI, SSDI, and Medicaid
   c. TVA, CQC, and HHS
   d. None of the above

10. Social Security Disability Insurance (SSDI) is
    a. available to the disabled family member only.
    b. paid out in an annual lump sum.
    c. designed for one who becomes disabled after he or she has a work history.
    d. not based on one's income level.

11. A Medicaid waiver live-in companion service helps in mortgage qualification because
    a. a live-in companion adds stability to the person with the disability.
    b. working with persons with disabilities adds stability to the companion.
    c. a portion of the companion's room and board costs are paid by Medicaid and can be counted as income.
    d. companion room and board costs are taxable.

12. Why are tax abatement programs good for a person with a disability?
    a. They lower monthly expenses of people on a fixed income.
    b. They make it easy to identify these people in the tax rolls.
    c. They are good public policy.
    d. What's good for large corporations is also good for people with disabilities.

Accessibility Issues

Learning Objectives

After completing this chapter, you will be able to

- Distinguish between adaptable, accessible, and universal design

- Describe the need for and concepts of accessibility

- List the principles of universal design

- Match prospective buyer's needs to homes you have to show

- List typical types of accommodations necessary for particular disabilities

- Locate resources you need for transportation, communication, and other accommodations in your community

- Prepare appropriately to show homes to people with disabilities

■ Key Terms

accessible design	basic access	universal design
adaptable design	reasonable	visitability
adaptability	accommodation	

■ Introduction

Have you ever needed crutches and discovered that it's hard to get in your own front door? Is there an elderly relative who wants to visit you but can't because your house contains barriers? Have you noticed how the world looks different when you are carrying a lot of bags, pushing a child in a stroller, or escorting an elderly person whose gait is unsteady? If local shopping centers can be built accessibly, why can't our homes? We want our relatives, friends, and neighbors to be able to visit our home and feel welcome, and we want to have access to our home during a temporary or long-term disability. We want to age in our home, not be trapped inside because we cannot enter it from the outside. In this chapter, you will learn about widely used industry terms and practices, including reasonable accommodation, visitability, accessibility, adaptable design, and universal design. You will learn practical applications of each.

Reasonable Accommodation

Do you use glasses for reading and a light to see your work? If yes, then you have used a **reasonable accommodation**. Most of us use these accommodations daily. If you went to a seminar and there were no chairs, you would complain. The accommodation of a chair would make your day easier. Most accommodations for persons with disabilities are reasonable and cost less than $1,000. Lower light switches, no-step entrances, voice-activated software, and wider doors all are reasonable and inexpensive accommodations. Both federal and state laws require that businesses make reasonable accommodations for employees and customers. Visit the U.S. Department of Justice Web site for more information on reasonable accommodation at: *www.usdoj.gov.*

Accessible, Adaptable, And Universal Design

Though the terms accessibility, adaptability, and universal design are often used interchangeably to refer to housing for people with disabilities, there are subtle, but meaningful, differences. Accessible design requirements can vary widely by state and local building codes, but with more states and municipalities adopting the Building Code of America and complying with American National Standards Institute regulations, HUD Section 504 regulations, and the Americans with Disabilities Act, accessible homes are part of our future. Additional requirements exist for buildings financed through federally assisted housing programs such as HUD programs for seniors or people with disabilities.

The United States Access Board has a slide show, "Understanding Section 504—Doing It Right; the Uniform Federal Accessibility Standards (UFAS) and the ADA Standards for Accessible Design," available at *www.hud.gov/local/pa/working/ph/504philadelphia.pdf.*

Accessible Design

Architectural **accessibility** involves details such as door widths, threshold heights, types of cabinets, lowered mirrors, special handles, larger rooms, etc. In contrast, access involves only two features: entering and exiting through one exterior door of the home without any steps and being able to pass through all main floor interior doors, including the bathroom (with at least a half-bath on the main floor).

The easiest way to remember the difference between accessible and adaptable features is that most **accessible design** features are permanently fixed in place and noticeable. (See Table 4.1.)

Table 4.1 | Examples of Accessible Design

■ Wide doors	■ Lowered switches and controls
■ Lowered countertop segments	■ Lever and loop handles on doors and cabinets
■ Audible and visual signals	
■ No-step entrances	■ Wall blocking for grab bars in appropriate places
■ Larger bathrooms	
■ Clearance for wheelchairs (33" minimum)	■ Installation of a roll-in shower
■ Knee space under sinks and counters	

Related to access is the concept of **visitability**, wherein basic features of access allow not only the resident with disabilities to move freely in their own home, but to be easily visited by friends, family, and neighbors who may also need access. This market of individuals and families need access to their own homes—and homes of others to be visitable. Visitability comprises a no-step entrance, wide doors and hallways, and a bathroom on the first floor. Some countries, states, counties, and municipalities are passing visitability legislation that requires new construction of single-family homes to be visitable. For more information on visitability see *www.concretechange.org*.

One reason that **basic access** is now required (Federal Fair Housing Amendments Act of 1988) in all new construction of four units or more is the understanding that a house is occupied not only by the original people who buy, but a series of future individuals who may buy, rent, or visit it for many decades into the future. The Fair Housing Accessibility First instruction curriculum, available through HUD, was developed by a team of architects and other Fair Housing Act accessibility experts to provide critical information on various Fair Housing Act accessibility-related subject matters.

To be in compliance with the Fair Housing Act, there are seven basic design and construction requirements that must be met:

1. An accessible building entrance on an accessible route.
2. Accessible common and public use areas
3. Usable doors (usable by a person in a wheelchair)
4. Accessible route into and through the dwelling unit
5. Light switches, electrical outlets, thermostats, and other environmental controls in accessible locations
6. Reinforced walls in bathrooms for future installation of grab bars
7. Usable kitchens and bathrooms

For more details visit *www.fairhousingfirst.org*

Adaptable Design

Adaptable design features are generally adjustable or can be easily added or removed in a short time by unskilled labor to adapt the unit to individual needs or preferences. An adaptable dwelling can easily be converted to a fully accessible dwelling, but accessible features can be omitted or concealed until needed so that the dwelling looks the same as other dwellings and can be marketable to anyone. In an adaptable dwelling, wide doors, no steps, knee spaces, control and switch locations, grab bar reinforcing, and other features may be built in. Grab bars can be omitted, but can be added easily when needed without opening up the wall because the necessary blocking was installed during the original construction. Installing a removable base cabinet face or installing self-storing cabinet doors that fold and slide back can conceal knee space. Countertops and closet rods can be placed on adjustable supports.

The American National Standards Institute (ANSI) standards specify adaptability criteria, which provide a full level of accessibility when adjustments are made.

Universal Design

Items and features that can be used by anyone, regardless of ability, are considered to meet the principles of **universal design**: the design of products and environ-

Figure 4.1 | Principles of Universal Design

Principle One: Equitable Use
The design is useful and marketable to people with diverse abilities

Guidelines
- Provide the same means of use for all users: identical whenever possible, equivalent when not.
- Avoid segregating or stigmatizing any users.
- Provisions for privacy, security, and safety should be equally available to all users.
- Make the design appealing to all users.

Principle Two: Flexibility in Use
The design accommodates a wide range of individual preferences and abilities.

Guidelines
- Provide choice in methods of use.
- Accommodate right- or left-handed access and use.
- Facilitate the user's accuracy and precision.
- Provide adaptability to the user's pace.

Principle Three: Simple and Intuitive
Use of the design is easy to understand, regardless of the user's experience, knowledge, language skills, or current concentration level.

Guidelines
- Eliminate unnecessary complexity.
- Be consistent with user expectations and intuition.
- Accommodate a wide range of literacy and language skills.
- Arrange information so that most important information comes first.
- Provide effective prompting and feedback in instructions during and after task completion.

Principle Four: Perceptible Information
The design communicates necessary information effectively to the user, regardless of ambient conditions or the user's sensory abilities.

Guidelines
- Use different modes (pictorial, verbal, tactile) for redundant presentation of essential information.
- Provide adequate contrast between essential information and its surroundings.
- Maximize legibility of essential information.
- Differentiate elements in ways that can be described (i.e., make it easy to give instructions or directions).
- Provide compatibility with a variety of techniques or devices used by people with sensory limitations.

Principle Five: Tolerance for Error
The design minimizes hazards and the adverse consequences of accidental or unintended actions.

Guidelines
- Arrange elements to minimize hazards and errors: most used elements, most accessible; hazardous elements eliminated, isolated, or shielded.
- Provide warnings of hazards and errors.
- Provide fail-safe features.
- Discourage unconscious action in tasks that require vigilance.

Principle Six: Low Physical Effort
The design can be used efficiently and comfortably and with a minimum of fatigue.

Guidelines
- Allow user to maintain a neutral body position.
- Use reasonable operating forces.
- Minimize repetitive actions.
- Minimize sustained physical effort.

Principle Seven: Size and Space for Approach and Use
Appropriate size and space is provided for approach, reach, manipulation, and use regardless of user's body size, posture, or mobility.

Guidelines
- Provide a clear line of sight to important elements for any seated or standing user.
- Make reach to all components comfortable for any seated or standing user.
- Accommodate variations in hand and grip size.
- Provide adequate space for the use of assistive devices or personal assistance.

ments to be usable by all people, to the greatest extent possible, without the need for adaptation or specialized design. (See Figure 4.1.) A related term is lifetime homes, a type of housing that allows aging-in-place—living in one's home safely, independently, and comfortably, regardless of age or ability level. The Center for Universal Design (CUD) is a national information, technical assistance, and research center that evaluates, develops, and promotes accessible and universal design in housing, commercial and public facilities, and outdoor environments, and in products whose mission it is to improve environments through design innovation, research, education, and design assistance. Considered the standard-setter for universal design, the Center describes the principles of universal design.

Many accessible and adaptable features are universally usable. For example, people with limited use of their hands cannot use round doorknobs, but lever handles can be used by both these people and those with full use of their hands. These handles are available in all price ranges, styles, and colors. Most people can reach light switches located 15 to 18 inches above the floor without bending or stretching, and this placement also allows easy access to someone who uses a wheelchair. By incorporating characteristics needed for people with physical and sensory limitations into the design, we can make common products and building spaces safer and easier for everyone, and therefore more widely marketable and profitable.

The universal design approach goes beyond the minimum requirements and limitations of accessibility law to thinking more broadly about how objects and space are used over the life span. In many cases, the client will have to make modifications to a property in order to live there. It will be a big help to your client, and may prompt them to feel secure making an offer more quickly, if you are aware of accessible properties. If you know about ways of financing modifications, such as ramps or lifts, you can help your client budget for modifications, which will in turn help them to make an offer more quickly and to secure financing for the modifications. Options for accessibility modifications vary from state to state; for an online, individualized assessment and links to vendors, see *www.lifease.com/lifease-livability.html.*

The booklet "Universal Design in Housing," available at *www.centerforuniversal design.org*, contains a complete listing of elements, features, ideas, and concepts that contribute to or can be components of universal housing. Click on Quick Links and scroll down to Universal Design in Housing.

■ Preparing to Show Properties

Be sure you know whether a property is accessible before showing it if your client uses a wheelchair or has difficulty with stairs. If the person has a primary caretaker, see if they can be present for the showings. In some cases, you will need to make special arrangements to show properties that may be currently inaccessible in some way but can be modified. Call your local independent living center for referrals for accessible transportation and interpreters, renting assistive communications devices, or temporary ramps.

When you have a sense of what the client is looking for, ask what kinds of accommodation they may need to visit the properties. (Refer to Figure 4.2 for types of disability and required accommodation on your part.) Be sure the client has appropriate transportation. If communication is an issue, be sure someone who can interpret will accompany the person. There are assistive devices such as TTY

Figure 4.2 | Type of Disability and Accommodation Required

DISABILITY	ACCOMMODATION
Deafness/hearing impairment	Use of interpreters, telephone relay, and TTY; amplified sound systems; captioned videos; advanced written materials for review before meeting
Blind/low vision	Accurate verbal descriptions of what is being shown; offering your elbow to guide the individual when he or she walks; different textures of floor surface; information in Braille or large print materials; pre-information on audio tapes; enhanced lighting and reading information to client
Intellectual or speech impairment	Careful, simplified conversations, asking assistance of family members, guardians, and paid staff to help the person understand you or to help you understand what was said; providing information in advance; patient listening, and asking for clarification if speech is impaired; communication boards with printed alphabet and symbols so people can indicate words by pointing
Physical disabilities	Accessibility features such as ramps, wide doors, and hallways; family or staff support; temporary ramps to gain access to potential homes to be shown; neighborhoods with flat terrain and curb cuts; ranch type structures and building with elevators; no-step entrances; accessible transportation; wheelchairs, which may be electric and operated with a joystick or by a sip and puff straw if the person does not use his or her hands
Age-related disabilities	Due to the nature of age-related disabilities, some or all of the accommodations listed above may be necessary. The individual may have sensory impairments, depression or dementia, and physical disabilities; thus a safe, secure, accessible home is necessary.

that you can use to facilitate phone calls with your clients. Other forms of assistive devices are often available through larger disability organizations such as United Cerebral Palsy. When communicating with a client who has a hearing impairment, the telephone company has operators as part of the Relay system to help you talk to each other.

■ What's Important to the Prospective Homeowner?

Like most people, a person with a disability responds to properties subjectively and emotionally. Your job is to help your client translate those wishes into the space of an existing house (or specs for one to be built) within their price range. What properties do you know of that you might be able to show? For some clients with disabilities, a conversation about the type of assistance they use will help paint a more accurate picture of the type of housing they need.

Beyond the emotional factors, there are basic practical considerations when choosing properties to show. Does your client use a wheelchair? Does the bathroom in a house you're considering have enough floor space so that it could be converted for easy transfer?

Working with a deaf client will require possible use of interpreters, writing to one another, or use of the 711 telephone relay. Working with a blind client will require a different set of accommodations such as offering your arm and clearly explaining the features of a home and neighborhood. Each client is uniquely different, just as each disability is different.

A term mentioned earlier, assistive technology is important here. It is defined as "any item, piece of equipment, or product system, whether acquired commercially, off the shelf, modified, or customized, that is used to increase, maintain, or improve the functional capabilities of individuals with disabilities." (29 U.S.C. Sec 2202(2). Every state has an Assistive Technology Office whose staff may be helpful in identifying local sources of assistance with modifications.

Costing out the needed accessibility conversions will help you and your client draw up a realistic financing plan. There are mortgage products from Fannie Mae and other lenders where you can borrow for accessibility modifications, but its best to think through how easily the modifications can be made before the purchase. For a state-by-state listing of Assistive Technology Offices visit *www.handiramp.com/ resources/assistivetech.htm.*

The need to make accessibility modifications, such as a wheelchair ramp, can also open up new resources. Think outside the box. Do you have a local chapter of Habitat for Humanity or a vocational school that might provide volunteer labor to build a ramp? Anything that brings down the price will help your client and a community project like this can be a neighborhood media event that again sheds a positive light on your business. For a comprehensive list of resources related to accessible housing, see ABLEDATA's Web site, *www.abledata.com* and click on "Resources" and then "Accessible Housing."

Industry Profile: Listing the Accessible Home

Tamara Eman, Realtor®
Prudential Georgia Realty
Atlanta, Georgia

I came into it by accident. I was listing an accessible home that took two years to sell, so I got to know the seller. I liked the aspect of going out to find places to advertise it and found many, many places to enter the listing and agent information.

That first sale made me work, and I liked the challenge. The home was very utilitarian looking—it had been modified with wheelchair lifts that looked kind of industrial and there was a roll-in shower in the bathroom. When I tried to market it to families with children with disabilities, I was surprised to find that other family members still wanted their fancy shower.

Eventually someone from Home Depot bought the house and put it back to its original state, but I helped the seller finance and build a new house. The experience led me to read a lot of publications I wouldn't have known about otherwise and to understand the vocabulary and the needs of people with disabilities.

Because there are few truly accessible homes on the market, in time I found these sales easier and quicker than the conventional ones—you're putting together a small pool of buyers with a small pool of sellers, so it's more targeted. If you've done your homework, you can spend a minimal amount of time with the buyer, as long as they trust your judgment. You can say, "I have two homes to show you, or, if you can wait six months, you can look at new construction." I've consulted with the Atlanta Association of Aging in Place and found that there are a few builders who work with universal design. I spend time on the phone calling builders and asking if they have lots that would be suitable.

Although I don't specialize in the area, over the 10 years I've been in business, I've probably sold 10 to 15 accessible homes. I like the mental challenge and creativity involved.

■ Chapter 4 Review Questions

1. An example of reasonable accommodation is
   a. offering your materials in Braille.
   b. removing an architectural barrier in a public accommodation when it is readily achievable.
   c. a no-step entrance.
   d. All of the above

2. Assistive technology is
   a. a computer-run appliance.
   b. the circuitry that runs special equipment, such as electrified wheelchairs.
   c. durable medical equipment used to assist people with disabilities.
   d. an item adapted or designed to extend function, such as a large-screen computer for individuals with vision problems.

3. Where would you be most likely to go for help in identifying local sources of assistance with modifications?
   a. Fannie Mae
   b. State Independent Living Center
   c. State Assistive Technology Office
   d. State HUD Office

4. "Universal design principles" refers to
   a. principles of design that are universally accepted.
   b. design features that make homes fully accessible.
   c. standards developed to guide design features that are useable by people of all abilities.
   d. design features mandated in the Fair Housing Act.

5. How can you best help the development of more accessible housing in your area?
   a. Educate your builders and developers
   b. Understand the financing concepts of SSI and SSDI
   c. There's no need to increase accessible housing today
   d. Rely on your customers and clients to relay their needs

6. Examples of universal design include all of the following *EXCEPT*
   a. an adjustable-height showerhead.
   b. floor-level electrical outlets in every room.
   c. pulls instead of knobs on cabinets and drawers.
   d. hallways and doorways that are 33" wide or more.

7. Which feature is required for accessibility in the Federal Fair Housing Act?
   a. Low pile carpet
   b. At-grade entrances on entry doors and apartment entrances
   c. Exact placement of light switches and door handles
   d. All of the above

8. Visitability means having
   a. no-step entrances, wide doors/hallways, and a bathroom on the first floor.
   b. lower outlets and the ability to roll under kitchen cabinets.
   c. motorized door and window openers for guests.
   d. nonslip flooring and textural differences from room to room.

9. An adaptable home is a home that
   a. has all the features needed for accessibility.
   b. is universally designed.
   c. will meet the accessibility needs of the owner, with some modifications.
   d. can be used for adoptions.

10. Which principle of universal design accommodates right- or left-handed access and use?
    a. Simple and intuitive
    b. Low physical effort
    c. Tolerance for error
    d. Flexibility in use

Strategies for Reaching People with Disabilities

Learning Objectives

After completing this chapter, you will be able to

- List five places where you can reach clients with disabilities
- Describe three strategies for outreach
- Explain elements that should be contained in your materials
- Research agencies and resources in your immediate area

■ Key Terms

accessibility assessment

ADA compliant

qualified lender

In this chapter you will learn about ways to determine your office's accessibility and strategize about how to market to clients with disabilities, including prospecting and marketing materials.

Buying a house is one of the biggest decisions many people make in their lives. Building trust with your clientele will be particularly critical to future referrals and can help you improve the public perception of the industry and connect you to resources in the community you might not have known about otherwise.

Working with clients with disabilities is a good reminder that advertising is just one part of marketing. Good marketing takes into account every aspect of your client's experience of your business. Do they feel invited in by your advertising? How do they learn about the service you offer? How do you present yourself as credible? How is the phone answered at your office? Is your office space inviting and accessible?

■ Is Your Office Accessible?

In thinking about accessibility, the best place to start is your office. The Americans with Disabilities Act requires basic physical and communication access to businesses. So ask yourself, Could a client using a wheelchair get into our office or have we made reasonable accommodations to serve this population in another confidential setting? Do I know how to use the telephone relay to communicate with someone who is hearing impaired? How does our office prepare printed documents for a client who is blind?

Title III of the ADA prohibits entities that own, lease, lease to, or operate a place of public accommodation from discriminating against people with disabilities. Businesses covered include hotels, restaurants, convention centers, sales establishments including real estate offices, offices of professionals such as attorneys and CPAs, etc. If a real estate broker or salesperson has a home office in which business is conducted with clients, that portion of the home must also be **ADA compliant.**

Another area to consider is sales of model homes. If a sales office for a residential housing development is located in a model home, the area used for the sales office is considered a covered place of public accommodation and must be accessible, although model homes and open houses are generally not considered to be places of public accommodation. The office of the ADA has stated that developers should voluntarily provide a minimal level of access to the homes for potential homebuyers with disabilities. For example, a developer could provide physical access via ramp or lift to the primary level of one or several model homes or, as an alternative, make photographs of the other levels of the home and of other models available to the client.

Several steps to remove architectural barriers to sales offices and model homes include:

- Installing ramps and making curb cuts in sidewalks and entrances
- Repositioning shelves
- Rearranging tables, chairs, vending machines, display racks, and other furniture
- Repositioning telephones
- Adding raised markings on elevator control buttons
- Widening doors and installing offset hinges to widen doorways
- Installing grab bars in toilet stalls
- Rearranging toilet partitions to increase maneuvering space
- Installing a raised toilet seat
- Creating and designating accessible parking spaces

Contacting local agencies, such as an independent living center, and asking them to conduct an **accessibility assessment** of your office for ADA compliance can be a good way to introduce yourself as a practitioner interested in serving this market.

If a leased office space is involved, determine whose responsibility it is to make various changes: the landlord or the tenant. The provisions in the lease governing the authority to make alterations will determine which party bears responsibility for compliance. For more information on ADA compliance and real estate professionals, see the ADA compliance kit available from the National Association of REALTORS®.

■ Getting to Know Community Resources

An important first step in reaching this market is to become familiar with resources available to you in your community. Use the table in Figure 5.1 to compile information about resources and contacts. This table can be removed and filed where you can use it easily.

Figure 5.1 | Community Resources

Provider Agencies

Agency	Contact	Address	Phone number	E-mail

Independent Living Centers

Agency	Contact	Address	Phone number	E-mail

Closest Developmental Disabilities Planning Council (DDPC)

Agency	Contact	Address	Phone number	E-mail

Closest University Institute on Disability (UID)

Agency	Contact	Address	Phone number	E-mail

Figure 5.1 (continued)

Organizations Serving People with Disabilities

Agency	Contact	Address	Phone number	E-mail
Veterans hospital				
Rehabilitation center				
Support groups				
Assistive techcenter				
Accessible transportation				
Accessibility modifications contractors				
Other				

Attorneys Specializing in Trusts and Guardianship

Firm	Contact	Address	Phone number	E-mail

Lenders with Special Mortgage Products

Firm	Contact	Address	Phone number	E-mail

Affordable Housing Organizations

Agency	Contact	Address	Phone number	E-mail

Publications for Advertising/Web Pages to Link to

Name	Contact	Address	Phone number	E-mail

Look up independent living centers or other social and human services organizations working with people with disabilities in your community and give them a call. Ask for advice on local resources: contractors who do accessibility modifications, interpreters, places to lease ramps, sources for accessible transportation, assistive devices, and so on. To see which lenders in your area are working with special mortgage products, go to the Fannie Mae Web site *www.fanniemae.com* and click on "Find a Lender Search." A **qualified lender** is one who has an agreement with Fannie Mae or other agencies to provide financial products geared toward people with disabilities.

Call your local housing authority/housing agencies to find out if Section 8 vouchers can be used for mortgage payments in your area, and if there are other local homeownership initiatives that might serve people with disabilities. All federally funded housing assistance programs are required to set aside 7 percent of the funds for persons with a disability—5 percent for persons with physical disabilities and 2 percent for people who are hearing- or sight-impaired. Besides giving you valuable information, this can also serve as your get-acquainted call with a group who could become an important ally and source of referrals. Ask if the agency has any homeownership initiatives and if they are working with any real estate professionals in the area. Then follow up with a thank-you letter, a business card, and a brochure. You might tell them about completion of this course so they know you have some background and are eager to work with clients they might refer.

■ Your Marketing Materials

This course has mentioned useful sources of information for your potential buyers. Display the materials in your office to make walk-ins and others aware that you have this expertise. Develop a packet for potential homeowners with disabilities that might include copies of the prequalifying budget sheet and instructions, sections of the Fannie Mae manual, and the table of mortgage products with local numbers. Once you've made a few sales, add any press releases or stories about sales to clients with disabilities, first asking the clients for their permission for the press.

Send out materials to disability agencies, nursing homes, organizations serving seniors, medical supply houses, home health agencies, hospital discharge planners, etc. If you work with mortgage brokers, send them the table of the special mortgage products you've learned about, and follow up with a call. For a listing of national disability-related publications, products, and guides, see *www.abledata.com*.

But, even before you have a sale to celebrate, let the community know via a press release that you have this new expertise and ask your new contacts at local agencies what publications they'd suggest you approach. Also, network with regional and local case workers, MS support group facilitators, contractors, and others.

Think about making your promotional materials more accessible to clients with disabilities. You might want to include a TTY number or include some other language in a prominent place referencing specialized expertise ("sign language interpreters available" or "accessible transportation arranged").

If you have a Web site, think of ways to make it accessible to visually-impaired buyers who use screen readers. If there is descriptive text that accompanies pictures of properties it will provide them access to this information. Although this can be time-consuming, there are simple alternatives and information available on the Web site *www.w3.org/WAI*.

When California REALTOR® Stephen Beard meets new contacts in the disability community, he puts them into an eight-week program during which time they receive materials via mail and e-mail, as well as two follow-up phone calls. After that time, those clients move into Beard's regular client communication program, receiving material on an intermittent basis throughout the year. Beard also hosts Accessible Homeownership Seminars, which he markets through area agencies serving people with disabilities and at disability-related trade shows. He has found these techniques helpful in "branding" in the disability community and driving new business.

Penny Payne, an Austin, Texas, salesperson was profiled in a *Realty Times* article entitled "Developing an Internet Niche for the Deaf." Payne first learned sign language to communicate with her aunt who was hearing-impaired. Although she is not deaf, almost 100 percent of Payne's clients have hearing disabilities. Payne sells about 25 to 30 houses a year and helps between three and five hearing-impaired buyers every month. For more information on the tools Payne developed to assist her clients, from special phone technologies to Internet technologies including a Web-based transaction and closing platform, see *www.realtor.org/rmomag.NSF/ pages/BEvans200106041*.

Celebrate Those Sales

As you get near closing, ask your buyer if they are comfortable with your developing a press release about them buying their new home. Whenever you can, include pictures in press releases about sales (with permission, of course). Remember that satisfied clients are your best source of referrals. A closing is always an occasion for celebration, but in some cases, provider agencies have also seen closings as a PR opportunity. There is a human-interest element to these sales that can make them mini media events and provide an opportunity for you to attract new clients.

The focus of any press coverage should be on the buyer's experience, but it can also be an opportunity for you to have your agency's name mentioned and to come up with a memorable, celebratory quote. Playing a key role in these purchases, you are in a position to offer a positive view of the real estate professional's involvement in the community. As New York REALTOR® Peter Staniels says, "If all REALTORS® did just one of these sales a year, we could revolutionize housing for people with disabilities more than all the government programs put together."

Figure 5.2 on page 49 shows one of Stephen Beard's postcard mailings. The information presented could easily be adapted to your real estate practice and your growing expertise with this market.

Industry Profile: Developing the Market Niche

Stephen Beard
Salesperson and Accessibility Specialist
Keller Williams Realty
Oakland, CA

I have built my business around service to the disability community. I think one of the reasons I have been successful is that there are so few real estate professionals that understand this market and know how to serve it.

I am a person with a disability. I have cerebral palsy (CP), which affects my gait. Before I became a REALTOR® I was a journalist. I had previously had two experiences with real estate agents—one good, one not so good—so I knew firsthand that there was a need to educate the industry about this market.

Ultimately, I'd like to see a special designation for REALTORS® working with people with disabilities. There is overlap between the two markets, but there are characteristics that differ with people with disabilities. Many people with disabilities are in the prime of their lives—they want to be active and involved—where the action is. You'll get a younger client who says, "I want that hip loft in that happening neighborhood—help me figure out financing for a lift or another accommodation to make that work."

The MLS in the bay area has special descriptive fields within accessibility, and I am hoping, eventually, for an online directory of accessible real estate salespersons. The market is there. The biggest barrier I face is the price of housing in the Bay Area. And specializing in this way, it will take time to build my business. For more information, please see the Web site *www.accessiblerealtornetwork.com.*

It is important for a real estate professional exploring any niche market to understand that the niche market requires an unconventional approach and it takes time to cultivate these clients. Mine is essentially a buyer's agency—I suppose I could have located sellers with accessible homes and then found buyers, but instead I've chosen to work with listing agents who allow me to find clients who will let me be their champion. It's more work upfront, but, ultimately, it's more satisfying.

The brokerage won't see the return in year one—many have policies around production and those brokers can't necessarily see the payoff of this approach. My brokerage agency is very agent-centric. From the very start, my colleagues recognized the importance of this niche ... and they allowed me the time to develop it. To achieve success, my critical path is to build allegiances within the community.

Starting out, I had to find the people in the disability community. Initially I advertised in the newsletters of organizations serving people with disabilities, and cultivated relationships with the executive directors of those agencies within a targeted geographical area. There is some altruism involved in my work—I donate 5 percent of the commission on sales to selected charities serving people with disabilities. As a result of this networking, I'm asked more and more to speak to groups. I've made presentations to independent living centers, a post-polio support group, and the Lion's Club. These invitations help with developing branding awareness and finding clients.

There are three components to my marketing strategy: direct mail and e-mail with consistent focus, regular public homeowner seminars and networking in the community. For each new contact, I send marketing materials and follow up with regular contact.

Business partnerships also make this work—I've built partnerships with key lenders serving low-income clients. I invited one of the lenders working with Community HomeChoice™ loans to speak at one of my regular seminars. She believed in what I'm doing and attendance doubled.

Figure 5.2 | Sample Direct Mail Postcard (front and back)

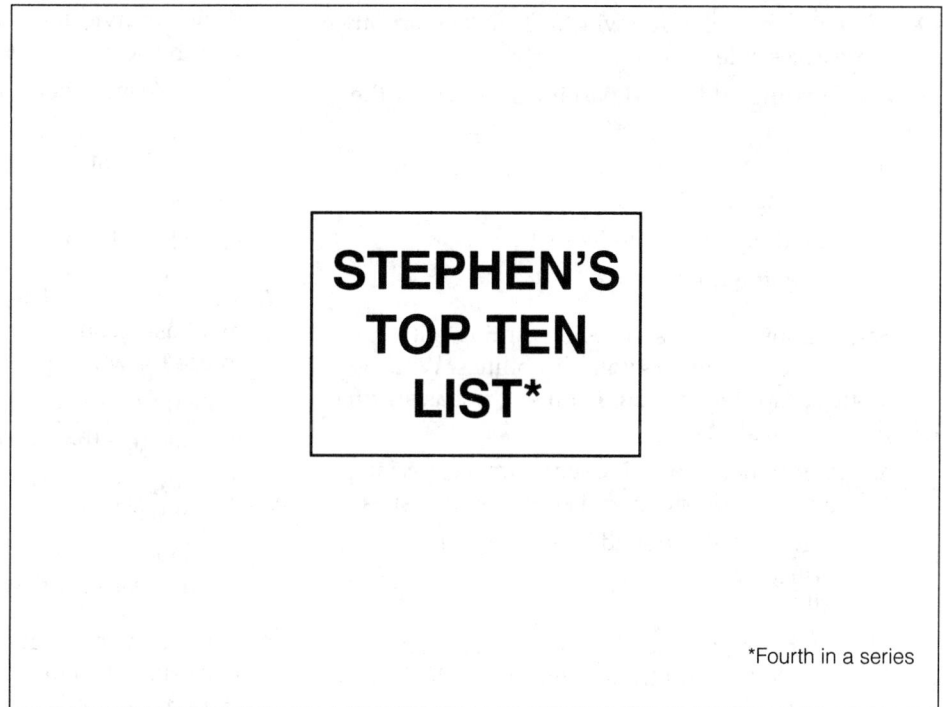

STEPHEN'S TOP TEN LIST*

*Fourth in a series

STEPHEN BEARD
Real Estate Consultant
Keller Williams Realty
4341 Piedmont Avenue
Oakland, CA 94611
510-364-6795

My Commitment is Your Peace of Mind

10 Tips for Hiring an Accessibility Expert

1. Look for a consultant who knows if homes are accessible BEFORE showing them to you.
2. Make sure your REALTOR® knows where accessible property is located in your area.
3. Investigate their special financing programs.
4. Ask if they know about accessible services in the community where you want to live.
5. Do they understand the renovations required to make your new home accessible for you?
6. Do they believe "Win-Win, or No Deal"?
7. Will they ask the questions that matter to you?
8. Trust your intuition.
9. Check their references.
10. See how promptly they return your calls.

Call me today to learn why I am your best choice!

Not intended to solicit properties currently listed for sale. Each Office is independently owned & operated.

Source: Postcard provided courtesy of Stephen Beard, REALTOR® and Accessibility Expert.

■ Chapter 5 Review Questions

1. Which of the following will *NOT* make your office more accessible?
   a. Creating additional parking spaces near the office
   b. Installing lively patterned carpet to prevent slipping
   c. Installing a raised toilet seat
   d. Widening doors

2. Salesperson O wants to begin working with potential homebuyers with disabilities. What strategy/strategies would you suggest as an effective way to start out?
   a. Advise her to provide seminars on special mortgage products and accessibility issues.
   b. Suggest that she send brochures to local service providers and follow up with a phone call.
   c. Tell her to research local disability-related newsletters and trade shows to see if she can pay for advertisements.
   d. All of the above

3. Which of the following is *NOT* likely to enhance your promotional materials to this market?
   a. Providing a TTY number
   b. Including your picture
   c. Tagging images on your Web site with text descriptions
   d. Including copies of prequalifying budget sheets

4. Which is likely to be the *MOST* effective way to reach this audience in a mailing campaign?
   a. Find clients through leaders at churches
   b. Mail relevant materials to discharge planners, trust attorneys, and service provider agencies, and follow up with a phone call
   c. Call the DMV and send materials to everyone with a special parking permit
   d. Buy lists from title companies

5. Because he works from his home office, REALTOR® Hector needs to make the home office compliant with which requirements?
   a. American National Standards Institute
   b. Architectural Barriers Act
   c. Americans with Disabilities Act
   d. Fair Housing Act

6. Which individuals will be helpful in developing your network to serve people with disabilities?
   a. Case managers and social workers
   b. Contractors specializing in accessibility modifications
   c. Executive directors of human service agencies
   d. All of the above

7. Your professional assistant with a visual impairment asks you for a specialized software program to use for work. What should you do?
   a. Purchase it for her
   b. Suggest that she purchase it on her own
   c. Suggest that she should consider another line of work
   d. Talk to the other staff about the issue and make a joint decision

8. You are the manager of model homes for a large real estate development company and there is a staffed sales office in each home. Which part of the home must be accessible?
   a. The entire model home
   b. The doors, hallways, and bathrooms
   c. The area used for the sales office
   d. The parking area and entryway

9. How might you remove architectural barriers to make your sales office more accessible?
   a. Add tables and chairs
   b. Position shelves within your easy reach
   c. Read the "Guide to Small Businesses" from the ADA Web site and call your local independent living center to ask if they'll do an accessibility audit with you
   d. Widen doors

10. How can you use your completed sales to market your services to this niche market?
    a. Ask for permission to take pictures at the closing and use them in your marketing materials
    b. Send a press release to local papers as a human interest story
    c. Send the press release with pictures to the local agencies you've identified as serving this population
    d. All of the above

chapter six

Case Studies

The case studies in this chapter are designed to extend the course concepts by applying them to real-life situations. Each case is unique and is followed by two questions for classroom discussion and two multiple choice questions based on the course content.

■ Case Studies 1–3: Your Customers

The following hypothetical prospects are typical of individuals you will be meeting as you incorporate what you've learned in this course into your real estate practice. You will be marketing to them, helping to locate houses that take their needs into account, assessing their finances and entitlements, and planning for their closings.

case study 1   The Davis Family

Ella and George Davis are in their 70s and have always taken care of their daughter Margaret, who has cerebral palsy. Ellen and George are people of means and have always provided for their daughter, including hiring a personal attendant who Margaret really likes. Ella and George own their home and their mortgage was paid off ten years ago.

Margaret uses a wheelchair and communicates through gestures and a communication board—an assistive device with symbols, letters, and numbers that she can point to. Her personal attendant helps her dress, bathe, eat, go to the bathroom, and transfer into the family car. Margaret receives Medicaid and is eligible for SSI, but has never applied because her parents supported her.

Mr. and Mrs. Davis want to be sure that whatever house they find will accommodate Margaret and a live-in personal attendant. They have a friend who knows a developer who has just purchased land for a small housing development near their home, and they want to investigate whether that community will include accessible units.

For Discussion

1. How can you, as a real estate professional, learn more about accessible housing?

2. How would you help the Davises and the developer in this case work together to ensure there will be accessible units in the development?

Questions

1. Accessible features

    a. are easily removable for future owners.

    b. are permanently fixed in place.

    c. require very little planning.

    d. refer only to easy entry to and egress from the home.

2. Supplemental Security Income (SSI)

    a. is designed for individuals with a disability who hold full- or part-time jobs.

    b. is designed to cover the costs of a full- or part-time attendant.

    c. is an annual benefit for all persons with disabilities.

    d. is designed for those who do not have a work history and are generally not able to work.

| case study 2 | **Norman Fredericks** |

Norman Fredericks is a 46-year-old blind attorney who suffered a spinal cord injury and now uses a wheelchair. Norman makes limited use of a personal attendant and is eligible for benefits. He does not take advantage of his entitlements because he is still practicing law and earns $180,000 a year. He is looking for a home because he recently became engaged and plans to marry soon. He wants a place that is completely accessible and visitable, and one that he can use for his home office.

For Discussion

1. How would you market your services to Mr. Fredericks?

2. Describe the features Mr. Fredericks will need in his new accessible home.

Questions

1. Visitability comprises

    a. a no-step entrance, wide doors and hallways, and a bathroom on the first floor.

    b. a bathroom and bedroom on the first floor.

    c. doors and ramps that accommodate walkers and wheelchairs.

    d. elevators for guests with any type of disability.

2. To get a better idea of Mr. Fredericks's needs and his housing price range, it is proper etiquette to

    a. check with his attendant.

    b. ask the income of his future bride.

    c. direct all questions to Norman.

    d. Address him first as "Norm" to establish a comfortable relationship.

case study 3	**Amy Barrett**

Amy is 38 and is a single mother of two girls (8 and 10). She has developed MS in the last five years. She is leaving the housing development where she currently lives because it has become unsafe and the stairs in her apartment are becoming increasingly hard to navigate. She wants to feel more settled so that she can live as independently as possible and raise her daughters. She knows that she will eventually need a wheelchair and someone to help her, but she does not receive any services now. She writes poetry and wants a quiet space for her computer. She wants to be in a good school district and have neighbors with children for her girls to play with. She needs accessible public transportation so she can get to her doctor appointments.

Although she does not receive services, she applied for Medicaid and SSDI and learned that she is eligible to start an individual development account. The IDA will provide a 3:1 match for every dollar she saves over a two-year period so that she can acquire assets to be used toward education, homeownership, or starting a business.

Her income as a clerical worker is $30,000 a year, and she has a Section 8 voucher.

For Discussion

1. What local, state, and federal real estate programs should you be familiar with when discussing housing options with Amy?

2. What accessible features should be incorporated into Amy's future home?

Questions

1. Social Security Disability insurance (SSDI) is

    a. for persons who have been disabled for most of their life.

    b. disability insurance to help with rental costs.

    c. for persons who have become disabled after they have a work history.

    d. not available to the disabled person's spouse or children.

2. Individual development accounts (IDAs)

    a. are administered by local/community agencies.

    b. may never be used toward a down payment on a home.

    c. are available regardless of income level.

    d. are an unmatched savings program.

■ Case Studies 4–9: Another REALTOR'S® Customers

The following case studies concern hypothetical real estate salesperson Alice Gregg and situations she encounters in serving people with disabilities.

case study 4	**Etiquette Issues**

Real estate professional Alice Gregg got a call from Bill Stewart, who has cerebral palsy and who was living in public housing. He disclosed that he received SSI as his main source of income. Alice found it hard to understand Bill over the phone and didn't initially think that he had the income to become a homeowner, but he was so insistent, she set up a meeting with him. She knew that she had a couple listings that had been on the market for a while and had motivated sellers, but she also knew that neither property had a ramp or other modifications to accommodate a wheelchair.

For Discussion

1. Where should Alice hold the initial meeting with Bill, and how should she handle the fact that she doesn't always understand Bill's speech?

2. Alice doesn't know if Bill has mobility impairment judging by this telephone call—can she ask? Should she assume he needs a ramp and go to the meeting prepared to discuss modification funding?

Questions

1. If Bill has a Section 8 voucher, what should Alice do first to find out if it's applicable to homeownership in her area?
   a. Ask Bill
   b. Call the state's cooperative extension service
   c. Call the local Housing Authority and ask for the person who administers Section 8 housing
   d. Call the Social Security Office

2. What are some likely sources that might be blended to qualify Bill for a mortgage?
   a. Section 8, SSDI, and welfare
   b. Special needs trust, food stamps, and hearing assistance
   c. SSI, funds from programs developed by the agency that works with Bill, and Community HomeChoice™
   d. SSI, Community HomeChoice™ loan, and, possibly, a Medicaid waiver, if Bill has a personal assistant who lives with him

case study 5	**First Party Trust**

John Milton was in a car accident and survived with a traumatic brain injury. He can no longer work and now receives Social Security Disability Insurance (SSDI) and Medicaid for medical expenses and ongoing support services so he can live in his own home rather than a nursing home. He received an insurance settlement of $500,000 that he used to create a first party trust to protect his eligibility for the Medicaid services he needs. With the proceeds from the trust, he may purchase a home for $175,000. The remaining assets from the trust will help him pay ongoing housing expenses not covered by his SSDI. Alice Gregg met John through friends and learned from him that the home he lived in prior to the accident no longer meets his needs.

For Discussion

1. How should Alice promote her services to John?

2. How can Alice learn about what resources John may have to qualify him for a loan?

Questions

1. How should Alice prepare to show properties to John?
    a. Ask John what accommodations he needs and whether he uses an agency that might refer her to a source for accessible transportation and anything else he may require
    b. Call the local independent living center and ask to rent a ramp
    c. Contact the local housing authority
    d. Ask a colleague to accompany her

2. How can Alice find accessible properties?
    a. Drive around and look for ramps
    b. Consult the MLS and make a list of those properties where Accessible? is answered Yes
    c. Contact local agencies serving people with disabilities
    d. All of the above

case study 6	**Third Party Trust**

Susan was born with a genetic disorder that has caused her to be cognitively impaired. Susan has income from Social Security Supplemental Security Income (SSI). She also receives Medicaid for medical and ongoing services to enable her to avoid institutionalization. Her parents are older and, as her guardians, they make any legally binding decisions on Susan's behalf. They have set up a third party trust with their assets to be used for Susan's benefit. The trustee of the trust is Susan's sister and the family has approached Alice about buying a condo for Susan.

For Discussion

1. What questions should Alice ask to establish who will be involved in the decision making process?

2. Alice has heard the family make references to the trust—what should she ask to establish the type of sale this will be?

Questions

1. What can Alice do to educate herself about trusts so that these transactions are easier and more clients with trusts come to her as the agent of choice?

    a. Develop relationships with local attorneys specializing in trusts

    b. Read everything she can find on trusts

    c. Spend a day at a law library

    d. Contact the state office for the Department of Developmental Disabilities

2. What does a special needs trust pay for?

    a. Medication

    b. Mortgage payments

    c. Expenses not covered by other benefits that contribute to the person's quality of life

    d. School tuition

| case study 7 | **Preparing to Show Homes** |

Alice is working with a client, Faye Wright, who had a stroke and now uses an electric wheelchair. Faye was very active in community affairs before her stroke and has become a seasoned user of accessible public transportation, but is frustrated that her wheelchair's weight prevents her from participating in many of her old recreational activities such as hiking and birdwatching. Faye has a live-in caregiver named Jessica, who she knew from her community activities and who can understand her speech, which is now quite slurred. Jessica is a little shy about speaking for Faye, but can interpret in a pinch. Alice finds it difficult to understand Faye over the phone.

For Discussion

1. What are some of the specifications Alice should use in choosing houses to show? Does the fact that Faye has a live-in caregiver have any implications for financing?

2. Sometimes Alice finds herself engaging with Jessica because she finds her speech easier to understand than Faye's. How can she keep her focus on Faye as the chief decision maker?

Questions

1. What are some questions Alice should ask Faye to prepare for the day of showing homes?

    a. How would you prefer to get to the property—do you need me to line up transportation?

    b. Will Jessica be coming with us?

    c. Are there any special arrangements I can make to prepare for the viewing?

    d. All of the above

2. What are some of the features to look for in properties to show to Faye?

    a. Stairs and a driveway

    b. Light switches set low enough to be operated from a wheelchair

    c. Door widths, adaptability of bathroom and kitchen, and an accessible yard

    d. A roll-in shower and low-pile carpet, or no carpeting

case study 8	**Modifications**

Mr. Carlson uses a walker, so an ideal home for the Carlsons would be one with no stairs. They asked to see a particular home in an area near their best friends, and the house has only one bathroom, on the second floor. The house is in a historic district and has a large, gated backyard. They fell in love with it and told Alice this is the house they want.

For Discussion

1. Should Alice try to talk them out of this purchase?

2. How can Alice find out about assistive technology that might help the Carlsons live comfortably in this home?

Questions

1. How can Alice identify sources of funding for modifications?

    a. Review the relevant chapter in this curriculum

    b. Call the local historical society

    c. Contact her local independent living center and ask for referrals

    d. Contact the independent living center and look at the Web site for the National Trust for Historic Preservation for information on modifying landmark buildings

2. What is the difference between accessible and adaptable design?

    a. There is no difference.

    b. Accessible design includes design features that can be used easily by people of all abilities; adaptable features cannot.

    c. Accessible features are usually fixed and noticeable; adaptable features are generally adjustable or can be easily added or removed in a short time by unskilled labor.

    d. Adaptable design means that someone in a wheelchair can use this feature easily.

case study 9	**Marketing**

Alice has now sold a few homes to people with disabilities and wants to develop more of these sales because she has found them personally satisfying. After years in the business, she found that making these sales tapped into her creativity. She is looking into how to effectively make her knowledge and services known, but doesn't know where to begin since the sales she made came to her by a fluke.

For Discussion

1. What relationships in the community should Alice cultivate to reach this market?

2. How should Alice go about ensuring that her office and her materials will attract this market?

Questions

1. What are the first three actions Alice might take to establish herself in this market?

    a. Read everything she can find about disability, check back with the customers with disabilities she sold to, and volunteer for the Special Olympics

    b. Ask to meet with her two buyers with disabilities to ask their opinion on how to expand her business in this market, compile a list of relevant agencies, and call to introduce herself and to get ideas

    c. Build a ramp into her office, put the universal symbol for "handicap" on all her materials, and enroll in an American Sign Language course

    d. Begin offering monthly seminars on how to do an accessibility audit, contact all lenders who offer Community HomeChoice™ loans and send them a basic packet introducing her business, and stop people with a visible disability on the street and give them her card

2. How can Alice work with her colleagues in the industry to expand her share of this market?

    a. Suggest that her brokerage offer a course as part of their professional development

    b. Develop a pool of accessible properties using the MLS and query colleagues about the particulars relevant to accessibility

    c. Offer a seminar on marketing

    d. Ask that they send any clients with disabilities to her

Chapter 1

1. **d.** People with disabilities can have adequate income for homeownership, they make up approximately 18 percent of the population, and there are many governmental programs available for assistance.
2. **b.** Homeownership provides stability and personalized housing not found in rental situations. Further accessibility modifications in one's own home are permanent and can be funded by government sources.
3. **b.** Working with clients with disabilities, their families, and local agencies will enhance your business by creating customer loyalty and increasing your potential client base.
4. **a.** There are approximately 50 million people with some form of disability, and over 150 million prospects when families, support people, and agencies that may be involved in the home purchase are factored in.
5. **c.** Because Americans are living longer and surviving illnesses because of available medical care, more people will have a disability in their lifetime; half who live to age 80 will have some form of dementia; half who live past 80 will have some type of physical disability.
6. **b.** The Americans with Disabilities Act mandates that businesses with more than 15 employees make reasonable accommodations for workers with disabilities.
7. **a.** People with disabilities were added in the Fair Housing Amendments Act of 1988.
8. **d.** Community HomeChoice™ provides underwriting to meet the needs of low- to moderate-income borrowers with disabilities or those who have a family member with a disability.
9. **b.** Budget-based qualifying is a way of determining eligibility that resulted from collaboration between the National Home of your own Alliance and Fannie Mae. It combines all sources of public and private funds as well as other staff support.
10. **c.** Both sources of information are helpful. Many MLS services have accessibility information. Internet sources quite often have a video of the home, which can be very helpful in determining accessibility options.

Chapter 2

1. **b.** The ADA defines a disability as an inability to perform one or more major tasks of daily life due to a physical or mental impairment. Such an activity would include walking, hearing, seeing, learning, breathing, caring for oneself, or working.
2. **b.** Treat a person with a disability as you would treat any other person. Ask rather than assume that a person needs help. Determine the disability and use common sense to act accordingly.
3. **d.** Trustees, parents, and/or guardians may serve as decision makers for a person without the capacity to make an informed decision.
4. **a.** It is appropriate to offer your arm to assist a blind person who is in an unfamiliar situation.

5. **a.** Resources for direct communication may include Relay 711 and sign language interpreters. It is important to discuss the importance of effective communications, particularly with a client with a disability, and to discuss resources that may be necessary for communication assistance. Just as with any other client, the real estate professional needs to fully understand the needs and wants of the prospective buyer with a disability.

6. **d.** Intellectual impairment, cerebral palsy, autism, epilepsy, learning disabilities, attention deficit disorder, or other neurological impairment occurring before age 22 are examples of a developmental disability.

7. **a.** People appreciate you being at their eye level so neither of you has to bend your neck at an awkward angle to speak to each other.

8. **d.** It would be better to use "Lee has a developmental delay" instead.

9. **c.** Guardianship is established in a case where a guardian (person, corporation, or public agency) is appointed by a court to act on behalf of a person not capable of making decisions. The guardian helps provide for personal needs and financial and property management.

10. **a.** The trustee invests the trust funds, pays bills for the beneficiary, reports to Social Security, and pays taxes on the income of the trust.

Chapter 3

1. **d.** Red Cross emergency relief is temporary housing assistance and would not be considered as income.

2. **b.** An IDA is a matched-savings program to assist persons with education, home ownership, or business start-up.

3. **d.** All of the funding sources may be used for accessibility modifications.

4. **d.** Funds from both A (Fannie Mae Community HomeChoice ™, Community Development Block Grants, and Supplemental Security Income) and B (Heating Assistance, Telephone Lifeline, and food stamps) can be blended to increase a person's income level.

5. **c.** Section 8 subsidies administered by local housing authorities may be used to fund homeownership depending upon the policies of the local authority.

6. **d.** All of the options listed are viable solutions to increase the resources of the individuals to afford a home.

7. **a.** A representative payee is an individual appointed by the Social Security Administration to receive Supplemental Security Income (SSI) benefits for cognitively impaired people for the purpose of paying the bills of the person with the disability.

8. **d.** A trust can be used to pay for all of the items.

9. **a.** The Home Investment Partnership, Community Development Block Grants, and individual development accounts are sources of federal and/or private funds for down payment and closing costs.

10. **c.** SSDI provides monthly income for a person who becomes disabled after they have a work history. Spouses and children can also receive benefits under this program. The monthly amounts depend on one's prior earnings.

11. **c.** A share of the live-in companion's expenses is reimbursed by Medicaid and can be used as income in determining mortgage eligibility.

12. **a.** Tax abatement programs help to lower taxes, thereby decreasing monthly expenses for people on a fixed income.

Chapter 4

1. **d.** Offering materials in Braille, removing architectural barriers, and a no-step entrance are all examples of reasonable accommodation.
2. **d.** Assistive technology is defined as any item, piece of equipment, or product system, whether acquired commercially off the shelf, modified, or customized, that is used to increase, maintain, or improve the functional capabilities of individuals with disabilities.
3. **c.** Every state has an Assistive Technology Office whose staff may be helpful in identifying local sources of assistance with modifications.
4. **c.** "Universal design principles" refers to standards developed to guide design features that are usable by people of all abilities. There are seven basic principles of universal design and guidelines for design that meet each of those principles.
5. **a.** By educating builders and developers you help them, as well as your customers and yourself.
6 **b.** Universal design electrical outlets should be installed at waist height, which is easily accessible for people who are seated.
7. **b.** The law specifies that one means of entrance and egress be ramped or made otherwise fully accessible.
8. **a.** The primary definition of visitability allows one to enter a home without a barrier, use a bathroom, and have doorways wide enough to pass through in a wheelchair.
9. **c.** An adaptable home is one that can be made accessible with modifications such as installing a ramp, widening doors, and installing grab bars.
10. **d.** The universal design principle of flexibility in use provides a wide range of individual preferences and abilities, including the accommodation for right- or left-handed access and use.

Chapter 5

1. **b.** Hardwood floors are easier to roll on than carpeting for wheelchair users, and clients with a depth-perception disability may have difficulty with a highly patterned carpet.
2. **d.** All of these strategies will assist a salesperson to develop their market and can be effective.
3. **b.** Providing a TTY number, tagging images on your Web site with text descriptions, and including copies of prequalifying budget worksheets all can enhance your marketing materials. Including a picture is not likely to have the same impact.
4. **b.** Mailing relevant materials to this group of agencies and individuals and following up with a phone call is most effective. The DMV will not share the information, and title companies do not keep disability related information.
5. **c.** The Americans with Disabilities Act requires basic physical and communication access to businesses.
6. **d.** All of the individuals working in the field of disabilities can be helpful to you as you establish a presence in this market.
7. **a.** A reasonable accommodation under the ADA would indicate that purchasing a software program is something you should do.
8. **c.** If a sales office for a residential housing development is located in a model home, the area used for the sales office is considered a covered place of public accommodation and must be accessible, although the

model home itself and open houses are not generally considered to be places of public accommodation.

9. **d.** Widening doors is just one way to remove architectural barriers that may exist in your office. The other choices such as adding tables and chairs or positioning shelves so that they are easily reached by you do not necessarily remove an architectural inconvenience.

10. **d.** All these strategies—pictures, press releases, mailings—will help the disability community identify you as the go-to agency salesperson for this market.

Chapter 6

Case Study 1: The Davis Family

1. **b.** Accessible features are permanently fixed in place.
2. **d.** Supplemental Security Income is designed for those who do not have a work history and are generally unable to work.

Case Study 2: Norman Fredericks

1. **a.** To be visitable, a home should have a no-step entrance, wide doors and hallways, and a bathroom on the first floor.
2. **c.** It is proper etiquette to direct all questions to the prospective homeowner, rather than to his companions, guardian, attendant, etc.

Case Study 3: Amy Barrett

1. **c.** Social Security Disability Insurance (SSDI) is designed for persons who have become disabled after they have a work history.
2. **a.** Individual development accounts (IDAs) are administered by local/community agencies.

Case Study 4: Etiquette Issues

1. **c.** To verify a Section 8 voucher, call the local housing authority and speak with the person who administers Section 8 housing.
2. **d.** The blending of SSI, Community HomeChoice™ loan, and the possibility of a Medicaid waiver is most likely in this situation.

Case Study 5: First Party Trust

1. **a.** Consult with the client and then fill in any remaining unmet needs through referrals from a local independent living center.
2. **d.** To find accessible properties, Alice should do all of these—consult the MLS and make a list of accessible properties from that source, contact local agencies, and keep an eye out for ramps.

Case Study 6: Third Party Trust

1. **a.** A good place for Alice to start educating herself on trusts is to develop relationships with local attorneys who specialize in trusts.
2. **c.** A special needs trust covers expenses that are not covered by other benefits, but which contribute to the person's quality of life.

Case Study 7: Preparing to Show Homes

1. **d.** It is important that Alice find out about setting up transportation, whether an attendant will be coming, and any other special arrangements.
2. **b.** The units must have appropriate door widths and an accessible bathroom, kitchen, and yard.

Case Study 8: Modifications

1. **c.** Alice should contact her local independent living center to obtain information on funding sources.
2. **c.** Accessible features are usually fixed and noticeable. Adaptable features are modifications that can be made quite easily.

Case Study 9: Marketing

1. **b.** The best actions to get established would be to ask to meet with her buyers with disabilities to ask their opinion on how to expand her business in this market, compile a list of relevant agencies, and call to introduce herself and get ideas.
2. **b.** It will help her to have a pool of properties that meet the needs of this market; this will also develop the awareness of her colleagues to look at their listings in a new way.

Accessibility assessment An evaluation, formal or informal, of how accessible a business space is based on the Americans with Disabilities Act requirement that all people have basic physical and communication access to businesses.

Accessible design Design features, usually noticeable and permanently fixed, primarily related to getting in and out of building if one uses a wheelchair or has limited mobility. Accessible design requirements vary widely by state and local building codes, and are outlined the American National Standards Institute regulations, HUD Section 504 regulations and the Americans with Disabilities Act.

Accessible REALTOR® Network An online directory currently in development by Stephen Beard of Keller Williams Realty, Oakland, CA, which will identify realtors around the country who are experienced in serving people with disabilities.

Accommodation The adaptation of a space, process, product or service to accommodate the specific limitations of a person's disability, (e.g., voice-activated software commands for people with impaired vision or TTY for people who are hearing-impaired are examples of accommodation.)

ADA compliant Follows all standards, mandates, and regulations in the American with Disabilities Act.

Adaptability The extent to which a space, process, product or service can be modified to accommodate a person with a disability.

Adaptable design Design features that are adjustable or can be easily added or removed in a short time by unskilled labor to adapt the unit to individual needs or preferences. An adaptable dwelling unit can easily be converted to a fully accessible unit, but those features can also be omitted or concealed until needed so that the dwelling units are marketable to anyone.

Americans with Disabilities Act (ADA) Short title of United States Public Law 101-336, 104 Stat. 327 (July 26, 1990), codified at 42 U.S.C. § 12101 et seq., signed into law on July 26, 1990, by President George H. W. Bush. The ADA is a wide-ranging civil rights law that prohibits, under certain circumstances, discrimination based on disability.

Assistive technology Any technology that assists a person with a disability to engage in the activities of daily living or participate more fully in society.

Basic access The extent to which a person with mobility impairment can get in and out of a given space.

Budget-based qualifying Using a budget of benefit payments, usually prepared by a service provider agency, allocating a person's entitlement benefits, to demonstrate to a lender that the person receives adequate monthly income to make timely mortgage payments.

Cognitive, sensory, mobility impairments Physical disabilities that limit a person's ability to think, see, hear, or move freely.

Community Development Block Grants Federal funds directed to local communities to be regranted to projects and organizations that serve the community's development, including initiatives targeted to people with disabilities.

Community HomeChoice™ program A Fannie Mae program based on a specific mortgage product designed to meet the needs of people with disabilities, particularly those receiving their income from entitlement programs such as SSI.

Court-appointed guardian A person selected by the court to act on behalf of an individual designated as not competent to make major decisions by virtue of a cognitive disability.

Developmental disability A physical, sensory, or cognitive disability whose onset began before the age of 22.

Down Payment Assistance Program A program that provides low-income people with money for a down payment on a house. Such programs are supported through a variety of federal, state and local funding streams.

Federal Fair Housing Act Passed in 1968, the Fair Housing Act is enforced by HUD and outlaws discrimination in the rental or purchase of homes and a broad range of other housing-related transactions, such as advertising, mortgage lending, homeowner's insurance, and zoning.

Federal Home Loan Bank provides stable, low-cost funds to American financial institutions for home mortgage, small business, rural, and agricultural loans. With their members, the FHL Banks represent the largest source of home mortgage and community credit.

Home Investment Partnership Program (HOME) pays for down payment and closing costs and/or moderate rehabilitation for first time homebuyers.

Housing rehabilitation The cost of modifying a home to make it accessible to a person with a disability.

Independent living centers were created by disability activists to offer peer support and role modeling, and are run and controlled by persons with disabilities and provide referrals and assistance to help people assume responsibility for their life and develop coping strategies.

Independent Living Movement began in the sixties, inspired by the Civil Rights movement and aims to improve the quality of life of people with disabilities by advocating for access to public areas such as city streets and public buildings, equal opportunity in education and employment, increased availability of adaptive technologies, and the right to have an independent life as an adult, sometimes using paid assistant care instead of being institutionalized.

Individual development accounts (IDAs) are matched savings accounts that community-based organizations, including the local area agencies that support people with disabilities, are increasingly using to help low income people build assets to use toward home ownership, higher education or small businesses.

Lifetime housing is designed to be useable over a lifetime, allowing homeowners to age in place.

Low-Income Housing Tax Credit (LIHTC) is a tax credit created under the Tax Reform Act of 1986 that gives incentives for the utilization of private equity in the development of affordable housing aimed at low-income Americans. The credits are also commonly called Section 42 in reference to the applicable section of the Internal Revenue Code. The tax credits can serve as a vehicle by which individuals with disabilities can lease a property for an extended period and then have an opportunity to buy at the end of the 15-year period.

Medicaid waiver program State program using federal Medicaid allotments to cover various services that help the person live independently. Waiver services are usually individualized to meet the needs of the beneficiaries and in some states the waiver offers coverage for the room and board expenses of the live-in caregiver.

Money Follows the Person A federal Medicaid program that allows persons living in nursing homes and other institutions to have their expenses paid in less restrictive living situations, such as their own home.

Multiple listing service (MLS) A service developed to assist realtors and buyers in locating properties for sale.

National Home of Your Own Alliance A federally funded national project established in the 1990s to demonstrate that disability and affordable housing networks could work with conventional lenders to expand the options for home ownership for people with disabilities. The goal was to create housing and support opportunities for people with disabilities through statewide initiatives.

Nontraditional sources of income Income that comes from some other source than employment, usually entitlement benefits such as SSI or SSDI.

Participation Full engagement in society through accommodation.

People first language Language that focuses on people rather than their medical diagnoses, thus "people with disabilities" rather than "the disabled."

Qualified lender A lender who has an agreement with Fannie Mae or other agencies to provide financial products geared toward people with disabilities.

Reasonable accommodation Title I of the Americans with Disabilities Act of 1990 (the ADA) requires an employer to provide reasonable accommodation to qualified individuals with disabilities who are employees or applicants for employment, unless to do so would cause undue hardship. Reasonable accommodation includes making a workspace accessible, modifying a process or tool or restructuring a job.

Relay The telephone company has operators trained in assistive technology as part of a relay system to help hearing customers communicate with customers who are hearing impaired.

Representative payee An agency staff person or caseworker authorized to access a person's monthly benefit payments to pay his or her bills.

Section 8 program A type of Federal assistance provided by the United States Department of Housing and Urban Development (HUD) dedicated to sponsoring subsidized housing for low-income families and individuals. Section 8 vouchers are issued by local housing authorities and make up the difference between market rent and what a low-income tenant can pay. In some areas, Section 8 vouchers can also be applied to mortgage payments.

Self-determination   is a movement in service provision that promotes people with disabilities (sometimes with their relatives and paid support staff members) driving decision making rather than the professional support staff at the agency that serves them. This trend has radically changed the way agencies do business over the last few years and has implications for home ownership as self-determination dictates that consumers, the people with disabilities served by the agencies, have more control over how benefits they receive through entitlement programs are allocated.

Small Cities Block Grants   Federally funded grants for certain municipalities often used to subsidize capital expenditures to improve quality of life, including accessibility modifications and assistance with homeownership.

Social Security Disability Insurance (SSDI)   provides monthly income for a person who becomes disabled after they have a work history. A number of persons become disabled during their work years from disease, illness, and accidents. SSDI is a social security insurance program that allows one to continue to receive income.

Social Security's Supplemental Security Income Program (SSI)   provides benefits for persons who have been disabled for most of their life, do not have a work history, and are generally not able to work. A person born with an intellectual disability or a severe physical disability would be likely to receive SSI.

Special or supplemental needs trust (SNT)   A legal, financial tool created for the benefit of the person with a disability to supplement government benefits and entitlements.

Trustee   A third party who manages a Special Needs Trust.

TTY   Assistive technology that facilitates phone calls for people who are deaf or heard of hearing.

Universal design   Design features that make usage easier for people of any ability, including those with a disability.

Visitability   A quality of design that makes a space accessible enough to accommodate visits from people with disabilities.

The Ten Commandments of Communicating with People with Disabilities

1. Speak directly rather than through a companion or sign language interpreter who may be present.

2. Offer to shake hands when introduced. People with limited hand use or an artificial limb can usually shake hands and offering the left hand is an acceptable greeting.

3. Always identify yourself and others who may be with you when meeting someone with a visual disability. When conversing in a group, remember to identify the person to whom you are speaking. When dining with a friend who has a visual disability, ask if you can describe what is on his or her plate.

4. If you offer assistance, wait until the offer is accepted. Then listen or ask for instructions.

5. Treat adults as adults. Address people with disabilities by their first names only when extending that familiarity to all others. Never patronize people in wheelchairs by patting them on the head or shoulder.

6. Do not lean against or hang on someone's wheelchair. Bear in mind that people with disabilities treat their chairs as extensions of their bodies. And so do people with guide dogs and help dogs. Never distract a work animal from their job without the owner's permission.

7. Listen attentively when talking with people who have difficulty speaking and wait for them to finish. If necessary, ask short questions that require short answers or a nod of the head. Never pretend to understand; instead, repeat what you have understood and allow the person to respond.

8. Place yourself at eye level when speaking with someone in a wheelchair or on crutches.

9. Tap a person who has a hearing disability on the shoulder or wave your hand to get his or her attention. Look directly at the person and speak clearly, slowly, and expressively to establish if the person can read your lips. If so, try to face the light source and keep hands, cigarettes, and food away from your mouth while speaking. If a person is wearing a hearing aid, don't assume that they have the ability to discriminate your speaking voice. Never shout to a person. Just speak in a normal tone of voice.

10. Relax. Don't be embarrassed if you happen to use common expressions such as "See you later" or "Did you hear about this?" that seem to relate to a person's disability.

The Ten Commandments were adapted from many sources as a public service by United Cerebral Palsy Association, Inc., (UCPA). UCPA's version of the Ten Commandments was updated by Irene M. Ward & Associates (Columbus, Ohio), also as a public service, and to provide the most current language possible for its video entitled *The Ten Commandments of Communicating with People with Disabilities*.

Center For Universal Design Housing Resource List

This selected list of Web sites will help you find information on topics related to universal design and accessibility as related to housing.

■ Floor Plans & Home Design

AARP Home Design
http://www.aarp.org/families/home_design

Architectural Designs
http://www.architecturaldesigns.com

B 4 You Build
http://www.b4ubuild.com

Design Basics
http://www.designbasics.com

Housing Zone
http://www.housingzone.com

Southern Living House Plans
www.slhouseplans.com

Universal Design.com
http://www.universaldesign.com

■ Housing Checklists

AARP Housing Checklists
http://www.aarp.org/families/home_design/rate_home

American Federation for the Blind, Environment Safety Checklist
http://www.afb.org/section.asp?SectionID=26&TopicID=144&DocumentID=191

Kansas State University, Creating Accessible Homes
http://www.oznet.ksu.edu/library/HOUS2/MF2213.pdf

■ Manufactured/Affordable Housing

Affordable Comfort
http://www.affordablecomfort.org

Affordable Housing Design Advisor
http://www.designadvisor.org

Cardinal Homes
http://www.cardinalhomes.com/buyer/aboutus.aspx

Dept. of Housing and Urban Development—Manufactured Housing
http://www.hud.gov/offices/hsg/sfh/mhs/mhshome.cfm

Excel Homes
http://www.excelhomes.com

Habitat for Humanity International
http://www.habitat.org

Housing Assistance Council
http://www.ruralhome.org

Journal of Manufactured Housing
http://www.journalmfdhousing.com

The Homestore
http://www.the-homestore.com

Manufactured Housing Institute
http://www.mfghome.org/default.asp

National Affordable Housing Network
http://www.nahn.com

Rebuilding Together
http://www.rebuildingtogether.org

■ Organizations

Advanced Design Institute
http://www.advanceddesign.org

American Institutes of Architects
http://www.aia.org

American Society of Interior Designers
http://www.asid.org

HomeSight
www.homesight.org

National Association of Home Builders
http://www.nahb.org

National Association of the Remodeling Industry
http://www.nari.org

National Kitchen and Bath Association
http://www.nkba.org

Project Action
http://projectaction.easterseals.com

■ Research

The Aware Home
http://www.awarehome.gatech.edu

Center for the Built Environment
http://www.cbe.berkeley.edu

MIT Age Lab
http://web.mit.edu/agelab

NAHB Research Center
http://www.nahbrc.org

■ UD & Home Modifications

Adaptive Environments
http://www.adaptenv.org

Center for Inclusive Design and Environmental Access
http://www.ap.buffalo.edu/idea

Concrete Change—Visitability
http://www.concretechange.org

Nat. Research Center on Supportive Housing & Home Modifications
www.homemods.org

Remodeling Online
http://www.remodeling.hw.net

Whole Building Design Guide
http://www.wbdg.org/design/accessible.php

Source: North Carolina State University Center for Universal Design Housing Resource List

Budget-Based Qualifying Worksheets

Appendix C contains the following:

■ A budget-based worksheet for hypothetical customer Joe Johnson, who has a disability

■ Blank forms that you can use when working with potential buyers

Sample Borrower Budget Worksheet

Name of Borrower(s) _Joe Johnson_

Prepared By _____ _Joe Johnson and Mary Johnson (mother)_ _____ _3/20/2007_

          (name and relationship to borrower)   *(Date Prepared)*

Name of Lender _____ _Central City Mortgage Company_

Verified By _____ _Jane Brown, Loan Officer_ _____ _4/3/2007_

          (name and title of lender representative)   *(Date Verified)*

MONTHLY INCOME ANALYSIS		CURRENT		PROPOSED
A. List Wage/Salary Income (GROSS)		170		170
Job at library				
Total Wage/Salary Income	(A-1)	$ 170	(A-2)	$ 170
B. List Benefit Income (Non-taxable) Supplemental Security Income (SSI)		988		988
State SSI Supplement		400		400
Food Stamps		120		120
Total Benefit Income	(B-1)	$ 1,508	(B-2)	$ 1,508
C. List Other Funds Designated Specifically for Mortgage (Attach documentation):				
Total Other Funds	(C-1)	zero	(C-2)	zero
D. Total Monthly Income (A)+(B)+(C)	(D-1)	$ 1,678	(D-2)	$ 1,678
E. List Other Sources of Support and Dollar Amounts or Value (these amounts may be included in income and expense analysis, but may NOT be used to calculate qualifying ratios—also, funds available for a specific type of support that are listed as income MUST also be reflected in monthly expenses on page 2)				
Money from Mother (Father's pension, documented)		200		200
Personal assistant funding support		1,600		1,600
Total Other Supports:	(E-1)	$ 1,800	(E-2)	$ 1,800
Total Effective Income (D)+(E)	(F-1)	$ 3,478	(F-2)	$ 3,478

Sample Borrower Budget Worksheet (continued)

Name of Borrower(s) _____ Joe Johnson _____

Number of Persons in Household _____ one _____

MONTHLY EXPENSE ANALYSIS	CURRENT	PROPOSED
G. List all living expenses:		
Food	340	340
Household Supplies	40	60
Utilities (gas, electric, water, sewer)	160	200
Property maintenance/repair	0	100
Transportation	100	100
Telephone	60	60
Cable Television	48	0
Clothing	100	80
Recreation/Entertainment	40	40
Health Care	0	0
Insurance (Health, Life)	0	0
Taxes (Income, F.I.C.A., personal property)	0	0
Other (personal assistance, child care, pet costs, gifts, donations, religious offerings—list here or on separate sheet and enter total amount)	0	0
Personal Assistant	1,600	1,600
Church Offering and Personal Gifts	56	56
Total Monthly Living Expenses	(G-1) $ 2,544	(G-2) $ 2,636
H. Monthly Bills (Debt):		
_____ (Joe paid off his one credit card during		
_____ his homebuyer education process)		
Total Monthly Bills:	(H-1) zero	(H-2) zero
I. Total Non-Housing Expenses (G) + (H)	(I-1) $ 2,544	(I-2) $ 2,636
J. AMOUNT SPENT FOR HOUSING		
(J-1: Enter current rent/J-2: Enter proposed mortgage)	(J-1) $ 760	(J-2) $ 840
K. TOTAL MONTHLY EXPENSES		
ADD (I) + (J)	(K-1) $ 3,304	(K-2) $ 3,476

Sample Borrower Budget Worksheet (continued)

Name of Borrower(s)_____ Joe Johnson_____

| INCOME AND MORTGAGE QUALIFYING ANALYSIS |

ENTER PROPOSED TOTAL EFFECTIVE INCOME (F-2) from p. 1   (F-2) $ 3,478

ENTER PROPOSED TOTAL MONTHLY EXPENSES (K-2)   (K-2) $ 3,476

from p. 2 (should include mortgage payment and all expenses)

L. Subtract (K-2) from (F-2) and enter here. This is your
PROPOSED RESIDUAL INCOME–NOTE: PROPOSED RESIDUAL
INCOME CANNOT BE A NEGATIVE AMOUNT   (L) $ 2

| QUALIFYING RATIO TEST |

ENTER (B-2) from p. 1   (B-2) $ 1,508

(i) Multiply amount from (B-2) x 1.25 and enter here   (i) $ 1,885

(ii) Add (A-2) plus (C-2) from p. 1 and enter here   (ii) $ 170

(iii) **TOTAL GROSS INCOME**—Add (i) plus (ii) and enter here   (iii) $ 2,055

ENTER proposed mortgage amount (J-2) from p.2 here   (J-2) $ 840

M. Housing Debt-to-Income Ratio: Divide (J-2) by (iii) and enter here   (M)   40.9%

(iv) Add proposed monthly bills (H-2) from p. 2 plus proposed monthly
mortgage (J-2) above and enter total here   (iv) $ 840

N. Total Debt-to-Income Ratio: Divide (iv) above by (iii) and enter here   (N)   40.9%

NOTE: PROPOSED TOTAL DEBT-TO-INCOME RATIO MAY NOT EXCEED 50 PERCENT
WITHOUT COMPENSATING FACTORS PER FANNIE MAE SELLING GUIDE

List any compensating factors or other comments here:

Source: Worksheets developed by the National Home of Your Own Alliance, and updated for this course.

Chart of Resources Joe used to Purchase His Home*

SALE PRICE	**$120,000**
Loan from Private Lender	$70,000
Second Mortgage from Housing Finance Agency	$20,000
Borrower's Funds	$ 500
Community Development Block Grant (City)	$ 7,500
HOME Funds (through city) Secondary Loan	$10,000
Grant from Division of Mental Health and Developmental Disabilities	$10,000
CLOSING COSTS	$ 6,000
Secondary Loan from Housing Finance Agency	$ 1,926
Grant from Division of Mental Health and Developmental Disabilities	$ 1,674
Service Provider Agency	$ 1,600
Grant from First-time Homebuyers' Program (County)	$ 800
REPAIR	$ 1,000
Church contribution	$ 1,000
REHABILITATION	$12,000
Grant from County Housing Endowment	$ 2,000
Federal Home Loan Bank (secondary loan)	$ 6,000
Community Action Program (CAP) grant	$ 2,000
Gift from Joe's mother	$ 1,000
United Way grant	$ 1,000

Note: This guide is dedicated to the idea that home financing must be creatively tailored to each person's unique circumstances. It is hoped that by sharing experiences and resources, you may learn strategies that will be helpful as you continue through your homebuying process.

* This table's purpose is to identify all of the possible funding sources a person may be eligible for. Every borrower may not be eligible for all of these sources of funding.

Source: Worksheets developed by the National Home of Your Own Alliance, and updated for this course.

Blank Borrower Budget Worksheet

Name of Borrower(s) _____

Prepared By _____
(name and relationship to borrower)   *(Date Prepared)*

Name of Lender _____

Verified By _____
(name and title of lender representative)   *(Date Verified)*

MONTHLY INCOME ANALYSIS	CURRENT	PROPOSED
A. List Wage/Salary Income (GROSS)		
Total Wage/Salary Income	(A-1)	(A-2)
B. List Benefit Income (Non-taxable)		
Total Benefit Income	(B-1)	(B-2)
C. List Other Funds Designated Specifically for Mortgage (Attach documentation):		
Total Other Funds	(C-1)	(C-2)
D. Total Monthly Income (A)+(B)+(C)	(D-1)	(D-2)
E. List Other Sources of Support and Dollar Amounts or Value (these amounts may be included in income and expense analysis, but may NOT be used to calculate qualifying ratios—also, funds available for a specific type of support that are listed as income MUST also be reflected in monthly expenses on page 2)		
Total Other Supports:	(E-1)	(E-2)
TOTAL EFFECTIVE INCOME (D) + (E)	(F-1)	(F-2)

Blank Borrower Budget Worksheet (continued)

Name of Borrower(s) _____

Number of Persons in Household _____

MONTHLY EXPENSE ANALYSIS	CURRENT	PROPOSED
G. List all living expenses:		
Food		
Household Supplies		
Utilities (gas, electric, water, sewer)		
Property maintenance/repair		
Transportation		
Telephone		
Cable Television		
Clothing		
Recreation/Entertainment		
Health Care		
Insurance (health, life)		
Taxes (income, F.I.C.A., personal property)		
Other (personal assistance, child care, pet costs, gifts, donations, religious offerings—list here or on separate sheet and enter total amount)		
Total Monthly Living Expenses	(G-1)	(G-2)
H. Monthly Bills (Debt):		
Total Monthly Bills:	(H-1)	(H-2)
I. Total Non-Housing Expenses (G) + (H)	(I-1)	(I-2)
J. AMOUNT SPENT FOR HOUSING		
(J-1: Enter current rent/J-2: Enter proposed mortgage)	(J-1)	(J-2)
K. TOTAL MONTHLY EXPENSES		
ADD (I) + (J)	(K-1)	(K-2)

Blank Borrower Budget Worksheet (continued)

Name of Borrower(s)_____

| INCOME AND MORTGAGE QUALIFYING ANALYSIS |

ENTER PROPOSED TOTAL EFFECTIVE INCOME (F-2) from p. 1 | (F-2)

ENTER PROPOSED TOTAL MONTHLY EXPENSES (K-2) | (K-2)

from p. 2 (should include mortgage payment and all expenses)

L. Subtract (K-2) from (F-2) and enter here. This is your
PROPOSED RESIDUAL INCOME–NOTE: PROPOSED RESIDUAL
INCOME CANNOT BE A NEGATIVE AMOUNT

| QUALIFYING RATIO TEST |

ENTER (B-2) from p. 1 | (B-2)

(i) Multiply amount from (B-2) x 1.25 and enter here | (i)

(ii) ADD (A-2) plus (C-2) from p. 1 and enter here | (ii)

(iii) TOTAL GROSS INCOME—Add (i) plus (ii) and enter here | (iii)

ENTER proposed mortgage amount (J-2) from p. 2 here | (J-2)

M. Housing Debt-to-Income Ratio: Divide (J-2) by (iii) and enter here | (M)

(iv) Add proposed monthly bills (H-2) from p. 2 plus proposed monthly
mortgage (J-2) above and enter total here | (iv)

N. Total Debt-to-Income Ratio: Divide (iv) above by (iii) and enter here | (N)

NOTE: PROPOSED TOTAL DEBT-TO-INCOME RATIO MAY NOT EXCEED 50 PERCENT
WITHOUT COMPENSATING FACTORS PER FANNIE MAE SELLING GUIDE

List any compensating factors or other comments here:

Source: Worksheets developed by the National Home of Your Own Alliance, and updated for this course.

D

National Perspectives: Design for Everyone, Disabled or Not

Reprinted with permission from the *New York Times*, January 7, 2007

By Lisa Chamberlain

Sharon M. Brown cried tears of joy the first time she took a shower without assistance in her new apartment. She had not been able to do anything more by herself than take sponge baths since she was hit by a drunken driver six years ago, further complicating the multiple sclerosis that had been diagnosed years earlier. For someone who had once hiked 100 miles of the Appalachian Trail, she never thought taking a shower would be such a milestone.

Ms. Brown's apartment building—which has bathrooms that are accessible to people in wheelchairs, including roll-in showers—is a milestone itself. The building, 6 North, opened in March 2005, and it was the first large-scale residential building in the country where all the units were built using what are called universal design principles.

While building codes set a minimum standard regarding accessibility, universal design is a relatively new concept that seeks to go beyond those codes to make the built environment usable by all people without the need for adaptation. This might include kitchen islands with adjustable-height countertops, front-loading washers and dryers, roll-in showers, and no-step entrances, eliminating the need for ramps.

But the important point, according to universal design advocates, is that it looks and feels like a normal apartment building. Rather than relying on designs that can segregate people according to their disability (impaired vision versus low mobility, for example), the intent of universal design is to create products and environments usable by as many people as possible, including people with no disabilities at all.

According to the Center for Universal Design at North Carolina State University, universal design is increasingly available, but few if any other large-scale buildings have used the concept throughout an entire building. The term "universal design" was coined in 1989 by the architect Ron Mace, who developed a set of seven principles, like "low physical effort" and "simple and intuitive use." Mr. Mace founded the center, in Raleigh, before he died in 1998, to further develop and integrate the principles into everyday life.

Colleen Starkloff and her husband, Max, who was paralyzed in a diving accident as a young man, wanted to build a national model of universal design. Through Paraquad, a nonprofit organization they formed in 1970, they had been searching for a developer who would undertake a universal design project. It was 2003 when Richard D. Baron, the chairman and chief executive of McCormack Baron Salazar, a nationally known builder of mixed-income urban developments, contacted them with what he thought might be a potential site for the project.

"He called me and said: 'I think I have a good site. How many units do you want to be universal design?' I said: 'Richard, I want all of them to be universal design. That's the point: universal.' And he kind of hesitated and said, 'O.K., we'll make it work.'"

Mr. Baron hired Andrew Trivers, founding architect of Trivers Associates, to create a mixed-use environment for nondisabled people as well as people with a wide range of disabilities.

The building is mixed-income as well; some renters pay market rates and others receive subsidies (one- and two-bedroom market-rate units range from $750 to $1,150 a month, while the cost of subsidized units depends on personal savings and Social Security income). In addition, there is a corner coffee bar, as well as ground-floor units that can either be retail spaces or private residences.

The building, in a St. Louis neighborhood called the Central West End, is 95 percent leased, with only 20 units occupied by people with disabilities, which is fine by Ms. Starkloff. "The whole point is integration," she said.

For Jacqueline Benoit, integration meant more than living next door to people without disabilities, but being able to live with and take care of her son Johnathan again. Ms. Benoit was on her way to work four years ago when a driver struck her car. After six months of intensive care, she was able to breathe on her own again. But the accident left her partially paralyzed, and she was sent to nursing homes for three years while her son stayed with relatives.

Ms. Benoit and Johnathan, now 7, moved into a two-bedroom, two-bath apartment in 2005, which includes subtle design features like door handles instead of knobs for easier grasping, a dishwasher and oven that are set into the wall and raised about 18 inches off the ground (a usable height for people standing and sitting), and a stove with control knobs in front of the unit rather than toward the back.

The design features make life more manageable for Ms. Benoit, but the building also offers something for Johnathan. "He loves the weight room," Ms. Benoit said. "We go together and I work on my arm. I'm happy to be alive and be able to take care of my son."

Before designing 6 North, Mr. Trivers had never used universal design principles, but now he is a convert. "This is the future," he said. "People are living longer and because of health care technology, they aren't dying from accidents and disabilities the way they used to. So the question is, how do you design so it doesn't look like it is for or is only usable by someone with a specialized need?"

Richard C. Duncan, the senior project manager for the Center for Universal Design, said: "Most people think U.D. is a term that is a synonym with accessible design. But it has this other element that is different: a social equity component. That is an invisible part of the product.

"So, for example, a ramp is very difficult to integrate into the design of a building," he continued. "We advocate for entrances that are step-free, that everyone can use, whether you have a problem with stairs or you're just carrying packages."

Mr. Duncan toured 6 North when it opened with other disability advocates and developers, and said the building was serving as a model. "And that is progress because what we don't want are one-off projects, but full integration," he said.

Most handicapped accessible buildings, he also pointed out, have two different apartment designs: "normal" units and accessible units for people with disabilities. "And neither are in fact very user friendly," he said. "The point of universal design is integration of design principles into all aspects of the built environment so as not to be obvious for one or another."

For instance, at 6 North, what looks like interior decoration is actually intentionally contrasting colors to allow people with limited vision to navigate the space. In the hallways, carpeting in front of apartment entrances is darker to signal the door's location. Next to each entryway is a small shelf, which looks like a nice design detail but is also a handy spot for people to put down mail or packages while they open the door. This is, of course, equally convenient for a parent carrying a baby or people with partial paralysis.

Jacquelyn Kish is one such person with partial paralysis, the result of a brain aneurysm and stroke she suffered 18 months ago. She moved into 6 North recently in order to resume rescuing injured or abandoned animals, which she was forced to give up when she was in a nursing home and lost her house as a result.

"I was told I shouldn't leave the nursing home until I could walk," Ms. Kish said while petting one of her rescued cats. "But I was determined to live on my own again. I can do that here."

As for Ms. Brown, living independently is more important than having hiked on the Appalachian Trail. "Being able to take care of yourself—you don't appreciate that until you're told you can no longer do it," she said.